Earth Science!
BEST
SCIENCE
PROJECTS

Planet Earth Science Fair Projects

Using the Moon, Stars, Beach Balls, Frisbees, and Other Far-Out Stuff

Robert Gardner

Enslow Publishers, Inc.

40 Industrial Road   PO Box 38
Box 398   Aldershot
Berkeley Heights, NJ 07922   Hants GU12 6BP
USA   UK

http://www.enslow.com

Library of Congress Cataloging-in-Publication Data

Gardner, Robert, 1929–
    Planet Earth science fair projects using the moon, stars, beach balls, frisbees, and other
far-out stuff / Robert Gardner.
        p. cm. — (Earth science! : best science projects)
    Includes bibliographical references and index.
    ISBN 0-7660-2362-1 (hardcover)
    1. Science projects—Juvenile literature. 2. Science—Experiments—Juvenile literature.
I. Title. II. Series.
Q182.3.G38 2005
507'.8—dc22
                                                                    2004010733

Printed in the United States of America

10 9 8 7 6 5 4 3 2 1

To Our Readers: We have done our best to make sure all Internet Addresses in this book were
active and appropriate when we went to press. However, the author and the publisher have no
control over and assume no liability for the material available on those Internet sites or on other
Web sites they may link to. Any comments or suggestions can be sent by e-mail to
comments@enslow.com or to the address on the back cover.

Illustration Credits: Tom LaBaff, except Jacob Katari, pp. 15, 49, 53, 58a, 60, 63.

Cover Photo: © Banana Stock Ltd.

Contents

Introduction

The projects in this book are all related to Earth, the planet on which we live. Although our solar system consists of nine planets and the Sun about which they orbit, the experiments found in this book focus on Earth and its surroundings. You will learn where Earth is located relative to its near and distant neighbors. You will also become aware of the vast distances that separate planets from the Sun and from each other. You will discover why our only natural satellite, the Moon, changes its appearance, find ways to keep our planet healthy, and learn how to make maps of Earth's surface.

Most of the materials you will need to carry out the projects and experiments described in this book can be found in your home. Several of the experiments may require items that you can buy in a supermarket, a hobby or toy shop, a hardware store, or one of the science supply companies listed in the appendix. Some may call for articles that you may be able to borrow from your school's science department. Occasionally, you will need someone to help you with an experiment that requires a subject or more than one pair of hands. It would be best if you work with friends or adults who enjoy experimenting as much as you do. In that way you will both enjoy what you are doing. **If any danger is involved in doing an experiment, it will be made known to you. In some cases, to avoid any danger to you, you will be asked**

to work with an adult. Please do so. We do not want you to take any chances that could lead to an injury.

Like any good scientist, you will find it useful to record your ideas, notes, data, and anything you can conclude from your experiments in a notebook. By so doing, you can keep track of the information you gather and the conclusions you reach. It will allow you to refer to experiments you have done and help you in doing other projects in the future.

SCIENCE FAIRS

Some of the projects in this book are followed by a section called "Science Project Ideas." These ideas may be appropriate for a science fair. However, judges at such fairs do not reward projects or experiments that are simply copied from a book. For example, even a detailed map of Earth copied from an atlas would not impress most judges; however, a unique meter for locating and/or measuring the intensity of earthquakes would certainly attract their attention.

Science fair judges tend to reward creative thought and imagination. It is difficult to be creative or imaginative unless you are really interested in your project; consequently, be sure to choose a subject that appeals to you. And before you jump into a project, consider, too, your own talents and the cost of materials you will need.

If you decide to use a project found in this book for a science fair, you should find ways to modify or extend it. This should not be difficult because you will discover that as you do these projects new ideas for experiments will come to mind—experiments that could make excellent science fair projects, particularly because the ideas are your own and are interesting to you.

If you decide to enter a science fair and have never done so before, you should read some of the books listed in the further reading section. Some of these books deal specifically with science fairs and will provide plenty of helpful hints and lots of useful information that will enable you to avoid the pitfalls that sometimes plague first-time entrants. You will learn how to prepare appealing reports that include charts and graphs, how to set up and display your work, how to present your project, and how to talk to judges and visitors.

SAFETY FIRST

Most of the projects included in this book are perfectly safe. However, read the following safety rules before you start any project.

1. Do any experiments or projects, whether from this book or of your own design, under the supervision of a science teacher or other knowledgeable adult.

2. Read all instructions carefully before proceeding with a project. If you have questions, check with your supervisor before going any further.

3. Maintain a serious attitude while conducting experiments. Fooling around can be dangerous to you and to others.

4. Never look directly at the Sun. It can permanently damage your eyes.

5. Wear approved safety goggles when you are working with a flame or doing anything that might cause injury to your eyes.

6. Do not eat or drink while experimenting.

7. Have a first-aid kit nearby while you are experimenting.

8. Do not put your fingers or any object other than properly designed electrical connectors into electrical outlets.

9. Never let water droplets come in contact with a hot lightbulb.

10. Never experiment with household electricity except under the supervision of a knowledgeable adult.

11. The liquid in some thermometers is mercury. It is dangerous to touch mercury or to breathe mercury vapor, and such thermometers have been banned in many states. When doing these experiments, use only non-mercury thermometers, such as those filled with alcohol. If you have a mercury thermometer in the house, **ask an adult** if it can be taken to a local mercury thermometer exchange location.

Chapter 1

Where Are We? Earth in Space

The giant sphere on which we live is our Earth. It has a diameter of 12,756 km (7,926 mi) and a circumference, at its equator, of 40,073 km (24,900 mi). Every day, at most places on Earth, we see a nearby star rise above the horizon, move slowly across the blue dome we call sky, and sink below the opposite horizon. We named the star Sun, and the time between one sunrise and the next is called a day.

The direction toward the horizon where the Sun rises is called east. The direction toward the horizon where the Sun sets is termed west. After the Sun sinks below the western horizon far enough that even the sunlight reflected by the air disappears, we are left in darkness. But the darkness is not total. Lacking the

Sun's bright light, we can see the dim light from many, many more distant stars. On some nights, Earth is illuminated by light from an object brighter than the stars. It appears to be about the size of the Sun, although much less brilliant. It is the Moon. Its shape seems to slowly change night by night from a mere bent sliver to a full circle and back to a sliver before it disappears, only to return again as a sliver. Like the Sun, the stars and the Moon in the night sky appear to move from east to west.

The distant stars seem to be in fixed places relative to one another. However, there are points of light that move slowly across the distant stars. Early stargazers called these points of light *planets*, from a Greek word meaning "wanderer." Later, after examining them through telescopes, astronomers determined that the planets were not stars. Like Earth, they are spheres that reflect the Sun's light but emit none of their own.

Seventy percent of Earth is covered with water, mostly deep oceans of salty water. Earth's dry land, which makes up only 30 percent of its surface, is divided into seven continents— North America, South America, Europe, Asia, Africa, Australia, and Antarctica. Some geographers regard Europe and Asia as a single continent, which they call Eurasia.

Earth's crust, on which we stand, is about 19 to 64 km (12 to 40 mi) thick beneath continents, and 5 to 11 km (3 to 6.8 mi) thick beneath the oceans. It is made up mostly of lightweight rocks (see Figure 1a).

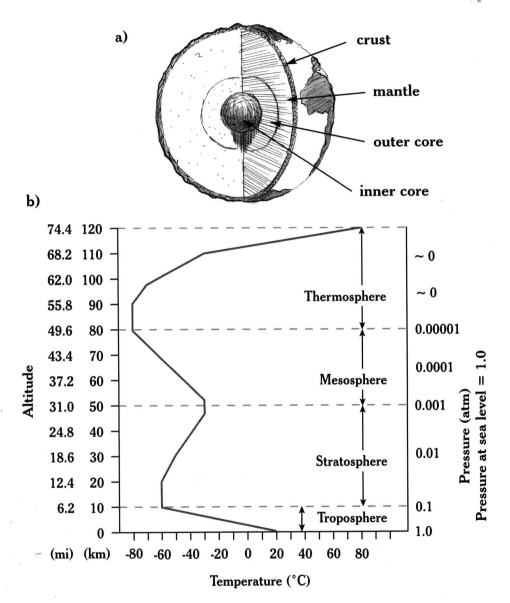

Figure 1.

a) Earth's layers are known by studying seismic waves. These waves travel beneath Earth's surface at speeds that depend on the density of the matter through which they move.

b) The diagram shows how temperature and air pressure change throughout Earth's atmosphere.

The mantle, which lies below Earth's crust, consists primarily of silica and minerals rich in iron, magnesium, and other metals. It is about 2,900 km (1,800 mi) thick and makes up 84 percent of Earth's volume and 67 percent of its weight.

Earth's core, which lies between Earth's center and its mantle, has two parts. The outer core is about 2,250 km (1,400 mi) thick. The inner core, extending outward from Earth's center, is about 1,290 km (800 mi) thick. The inner core is believed to be mostly solid iron together with some other dense elements such as nickel. The same materials make up the outer core, which seems to be liquid.

Above the planet's surface lies an atmosphere of air that contains enough oxygen to make life possible. We live at the bottom of that ocean of air, most of which is within 100 km (62 mi) of Earth's crust, as shown in Figure 1b. The troposphere, the first 11 km (7 mi) of air above the surface, is where we live and where weather takes place. As we ascend into the troposphere, air temperature and pressure decrease. However, in the stratosphere, the temperature of the very thin air rises, only to fall again in the mesosphere. The stratosphere has a layer of ozone that absorbs much of the Sun's dangerous ultraviolet radiation. Temperatures decline through the mesosphere, then rise again in the thermosphere.

Not shown in the diagram is the ionosphere, which extends from 48 to 400 km (30 to 250 mi) above Earth's surface.

In the ionosphere, air molecules are ionized (changed to charged particles) by the Sun's radiation. The ionosphere reflects radio waves, making radio communication possible over long distances. Unaware that the ionosphere existed, Thomas Edison predicted that Guglielmo Marconi's attempt to send radio waves across the ocean from North America to England would fail. He believed that Earth's curvature would cause radio waves to move along a straight path into outer space. Marconi had evidence that radio waves were reflected by something in the atmosphere. Much to Edison's astonishment, Marconi was successful in establishing long-range communication using electromagnetic waves.

Experiment 1.1

Air Pressure, Temperature, and Altitude

Materials

✓ **an adult**

✓ outdoor thermometer

✓ pen or pencil and notebook

✓ aneroid barometer

✓ mountain

Pressure is defined as force per area. When you stand on a floor, your entire weight (a force) pushes on an area equal to the area of your feet. If you weigh 50 kg (110 lb) and the area of your shoes is 400 cm^2 (62 in^2), the pressure you exert on the floor is

$$\frac{50 \text{ kg}}{400 \text{ cm}^2} = 0.125 \text{ kg/cm}^2 \quad \text{or} \quad \frac{110 \text{ lb}}{62 \text{ in}^2} = 1.77 \text{ lb/in}^2$$

Since we live at the bottom of an ocean of air, there is a long column of air above us. Like you, that tall column of air has weight. The air's weight pushes against you and everything else, just as your weight pushes on a floor when you stand on it.

Based on what you just read, and on Figure 1b, what would you expect to happen to the pressure exerted by air as you ascend a mountain? What would you expect to happen to the temperature of the air as you ascend a mountain?

To check your predictions, use a thermometer to measure air temperature at the base of a mountain. Record that temperature. At the same time, use an aneroid barometer to measure air pressure at the base of the mountain.

An aneroid barometer (Figure 2a) has a hole in the back where air can enter. The air pushes against a sealed, thin, hollow metal can from which most of the air has been removed. The outside of the can is attached to a spring. A series of levers connects the spring to a chain that turns a pointer over the barometer's dial, shown in Figure 2b. Often there will be a needle that can be set by hand so that you can see whether the pressure is increasing or decreasing over time.

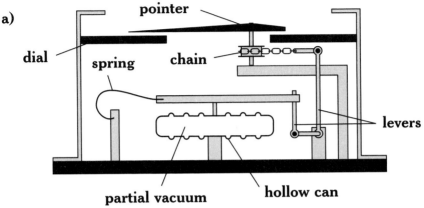

a)

pointer

dial

spring

chain

levers

partial vacuum

hollow can

b)

needle that can be turned by hand

needle that can indicate pressure on dial

Figure 2.

a) A side-view diagram of an aneroid barometer.
b) The dial of an aneroid barometer, which allows you to measure air pressure. Most aneroid barometers show pressure in inches of mercury. Normal atmospheric pressure at sea level is 30 inches of mercury, which is the same as 14.7 pounds per square inch or 1.04 kilograms per square centimeter.

When air pressure increases, the sides of the can are pushed inward, stretching the spring. The spring pulls on the chain, turning the pointer toward a larger number on the dial. When air pressure decreases, the sides of the can move outward, the spring is under less tension. The pointer moves back to a smaller number on the dial.

With **an adult**, travel to the top of the mountain and again measure and record the air temperature and pressure. Do your results confirm your prediction? How might differences in time of day at the base and top of the mountain affect your measurements?

If you know the altitude at the top and base of the mountain, how can you estimate the change in pressure and temperature per meter (or foot) of altitude?

If there are no mountains nearby, you could carry the barometer from the basement of a tall building to the top of the same building. How many floors do you have to ascend before you can detect a change in air pressure?

If you live in a multistory house or apartment, can you detect a change in pressure between the bottom and top floors of the house or apartment?

Science Project Ideas

- Do some research on Blaise Pascal (1623–1662), a French mathematician and physicist. What experiment did Pascal perform at the Puy de Dôme in France in 1648? What led him to perform this experiment? Can you duplicate it using an aneroid barometer?

- Who was Evangelista Torricelli (1608–1647) and what did he invent? For what discovery is he famous? Can you duplicate his experiment using water?

- As you ascend a mountain or take off in an airplane, do you often sense a strange feeling in your ears? Can that feeling be eliminated by swallowing or moving your jaw? How can you explain the strange feeling? How might swallowing or moving your jaw return your ears to normal?

Experiment 1.2

Pressure, Temperature, and Depth

Materials

- ✓ **an adult**
- ✓ aneroid barometer
- ✓ clear plastic bag
- ✓ pail
- ✓ water, cold and warm
- ✓ deep lake or pond
- ✓ boat and life vests
- ✓ thermometer (⁻10°C–110°C)

- ✓ a weight such as a lead sinker
- ✓ long piece of fishing line
- ✓ string
- ✓ watch
- ✓ eyedropper
- ✓ food coloring
- ✓ 2 clear plastic vials or small drinking glasses

Pressure and Depth

Not only are there pressure changes as you ascend or descend in the atmosphere, but there are also pressure differences at different depths of water. When you dive into a swimming pool, you can probably feel a change in pressure in your ears. To see how pressure changes with the depth of the water, place an aneroid barometer in a clear plastic bag. Seal the bag so that water cannot enter it. Then lower the enclosed barometer into a pail of water. What happens to the pressure inside the bag as you lower it deeper into the water? How can you explain the change in pressure?

Temperature and Depth

Ask an adult to help you with this experiment. To see the effect of water depth on temperature, you will need some deep water, such as a lake or pond. **Accompanied by an adult and wearing life vests,** take a boat to the center of a deep lake or pond. Use a thermometer to measure the temperature of the water at the pond's surface.

Tie a weight to the end of a long piece of fishing line. Tie the thermometer to the weight or line. Lower the line into the water so that the thermometer is carried deep down into the pond. After five minutes, quickly raise the thermometer and read the thermometer. How does the depth of the water affect its temperature?

To see why the temperature changes with depth, you will need an eyedropper, food coloring, two clear plastic vials or small drinking glasses, and warm and cold water. Place a drop of food coloring in one vial or glass. Nearly fill that vial with cold water. Add a similar amount of warm water

cold water

warm water

Figure 3.

What happens when a drop of cold water is placed in warm water? Is the density of water affected by temperature?

to the second vial or glass. Next, use the eyedropper to remove some of the cold colored water. Place the end of the eyedropper just below the surface of the warm water, as shown in Figure 3. Slowly squeeze the bulb of the eyedropper so that a small amount of cold colored water enters the warm water. What happens to the cold water? Does it rise or sink or stay where you put it? What does this tell you about the density (weight per volume) of cold water, as compared with warm water?

How does this experiment help explain why the temperature of water is related to its depth in a lake or pond?

Science Project Ideas

- If cold water is denser than warm water, why does ice float? Is there some temperature at which the density of colder water becomes less than that of warmer water? If so, what is that temperature? Can you offer experimental evidence for such a temperature?

- How does the pressure at the deepest point in the Pacific Ocean (11,033 m, or 36,198 ft) compare with the pressure of the atmosphere at Earth's surface?

- There is no air on the Moon, so the Moon's surface is in a very good vacuum. How did astronauts who walked on the Moon manage to survive in such a vacuum?

Experiment 1.3

Evidence for a Spherical Earth

Materials

- ✓ lamp with lightbulb
- ✓ dark room
- ✓ sphere such as a soccer ball or beach ball
- ✓ Frisbee or a jar lid
- ✓ cylinder, such as an aluminum can
- ✓ cone-shaped object

Ancient sailors often avoided sailing beyond sight of land. They feared they would fall off the edge of what they believed was a disk-shaped Earth. You have probably seen photographs of Earth taken from space or from the Moon's surface. Such photographs provide convincing evidence that Earth is a sphere. But these photographs did not surprise anyone. People have known for centuries that we live on a sphere. Although ancient sailors believed that Earth was flat, astronomers and geographers of the same era knew Earth was round. How did they know?

Aristotle (384–322 B.C.), a famous Greek philosopher, offered evidence of Earth's spherical shape. He noticed that during an eclipse of the Moon, the edge of Earth's shadow could be seen on the lunar surface. That shadow was always curved. Aristotle argued that only a sphere can cast a shadow that is always round. Is this true?

To find out, place a single lightbulb near one side of an otherwise dark room. The bulb will be used to cast shadows of objects held near a wall on the opposite side of the room.

Begin with a sphere such as a soccer or beach ball. Hold the sphere near the wall and turn it in various ways. Does the sphere always cast a round shadow?

Are there other shapes that will always cast round shadows? To find out, test for a disk-shaped Earth using a Frisbee or a jar lid. Can you hold the disk so that it casts a round shadow? Can the disk cast shadows that are not round? If so, how many different shadow shapes can it cast?

Use a cylinder, such as an aluminum can, to cast shadows. Can a cylinder cast a round shadow? Can it cast shadows with other shapes? If so, how many differently shaped shadows can it cast?

How about a cone? Can it cast a round shadow? Can it cast shadows with other shapes? If so, how many different shadow shapes can it cast? What other objects might cast round shadows? Do these objects *always* cast a round shadow?

Aristotle also noted that sailors on ships sailing northward would observe previously unseen stars appear on the northern horizon, while stars on the southern horizon disappeared. The opposite was true when they sailed southward. As Figure 4 demonstrates, this effect could easily be explained by a spherical Earth.

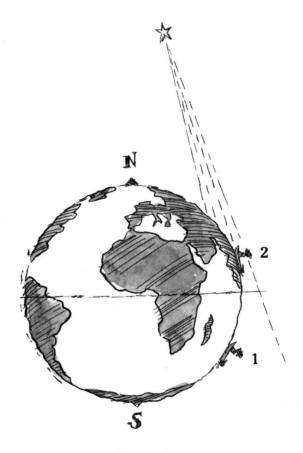

Figure 4.

At position 1 on a spherical Earth, the light from a certain star cannot be seen. By moving north to position 2, the star becomes visible. Its light is no longer blocked by Earth.

Perhaps you have noticed that on a clear day, if you look across the sea to the horizon, an incoming ship's mast and sails will be seen before its hull. Do you see how a spherical Earth can explain why the taller parts of a ship appear first as it sails toward you?

EARTH'S IMAGINARY GRID AND A CANOPY OF STARS

Positions on Earth are established from a giant imaginary grid (see Figure 5) that covers the planet's surface. These are the lines you see on a world map or a globe. The lines that run from the North Pole to the South Pole are called meridians. These lines measure longitude. The prime meridian is zero degrees longitude. It passes through Greenwich, England. If you look on a globe, you will see that the distance between these longitude lines is greatest at the equator. The lines join to form a point at each pole. Because there are 360 degrees in a circle and 24 hours in one day (one revolution of Earth), the major meridian lines are 15 degrees apart ($360° \div 24$ hr = $15°$/hr). This is also why time zones are about 15 degrees apart. For political and economic reasons, time zones in many countries are not exactly 15 degrees apart.

When you move westward from one time zone to the next, you set your clock back one hour.

Imaginary lines parallel to the equator are called parallels. They are used to measure latitude—degrees north or south of the equator. Degrees of latitude are about 111 km (69 mi) apart. The North Pole is 90 degrees latitude. The equator is 0 degrees latitude. How far is it from the North Pole to the equator?

When you look up at the night sky, you see hundreds of stars spread out over what looks to be a slightly flattened dome.

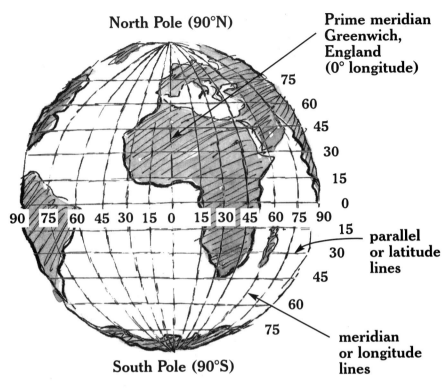

Figure 5.

We use an imaginary grid over Earth to pinpoint locations. Meridians, lines of longitude, give us our east-west position. Parallels, lines of latitude, give us our north-south position. Philadelphia is approximately 75° west of Greenwich England, which is 0° longitude, and 40° north of the equator, which is 0° latitude. Can you find it on a globe?

This canopy of stars is known as the celestial sphere. We can use the stars in the celestial sphere to determine our position on Earth. You will see how we do that in Experiment 1.5. But first, you need to know something about the light that comes from stars.

Experiment 1.4

The Light From Stars

Materials

✓ clear lightbulb with a line filament

✓ socket for bulb

✓ straight pins

✓ sheet of cardboard

✓ dark room

✓ sunlight

Figure 6 shows you how a clear lightbulb with a line filament can be used to represent a star. The bulb is placed in a socket and turned so that the end of the filament is turned toward you. The end of the filament is just a point of light. The same is true of a distant star. It is just a small dot set in the dark sky.

Stick three common pins side by side and about a centimeter apart at one end of a sheet of cardboard. If you hold the pins close to the point of light, you will see that the shadows of the pins diverge (spread apart). But what happens as you move the pins farther from the light?

As you have just seen, light rays from a source of light that is far away are parallel (or very nearly so) and, therefore, the pins cast parallel shadows. What do you think will happen if these three pins are placed in sunlight? Do you think their shadows will be parallel?

Try it! Were you right?

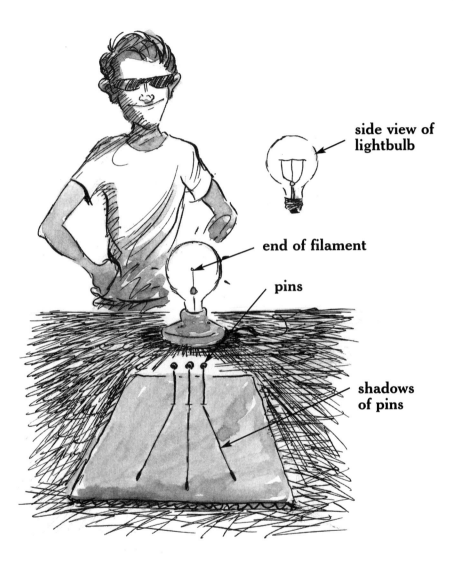

side view of
lightbulb

end of filament

pins

shadows
of pins

Figure 6.

The end of a line filament looks like a point of light. It can be
used to represent light from a star. Shadows of pins can
be used to show that light rays reaching Earth from a distant
star are parallel.

Science Project Ideas

- What is the definition of *parallax*? Design an experiment to demonstrate parallax. How is parallax used to measure the distance to stars?

- Design and carry out an experiment to estimate the number of all the stars that are visible in the night sky.

Experiment 1.5

Using a Star to Find Your Latitude

Materials

✓ a clear night   ✓ a helper

✓ astrolabe (see Figure 8b)

Do you know the latitude where you live? You can find your latitude by measuring the altitude of the North Star (Polaris), which is located almost directly above Earth's North Pole. As you can see from Figure 7, the altitude of Polaris (its angle of elevation above the horizon) is equal to the latitude from which its altitude is measured. At the North Pole, latitude 90 degrees, it is directly overhead, an altitude of 90 degrees. At

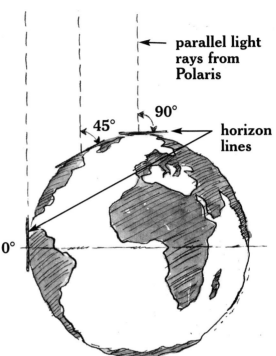

Figure 7.

You can find your latitude. It is equal to the altitude of the North Star (Polaris). Horizons in the diagram are shown as lines that are parallel to Earth's surface.

the equator, latitude 0 degrees, it is on the horizon, an altitude of 0 degrees. At a latitude of 45 degrees, the altitude of Polaris is 45 degrees.

Because Polaris is so far from Earth, light rays coming from the star are parallel, as you found they would be in the previous experiment. Any light rays that were not parallel would not hit Earth.

To find Polaris, go outside on a clear night. Look to the northern half of the sky to find the Big Dipper. It consists of a group of bright stars that look like the side of a cooking pan, as shown in Figure 8a. Depending on the season and the time of night, the Big Dipper may be turned at different angles in the sky. The pointer stars, Dubhe and Merak, form a line that always points toward Polaris. The distance from Polaris to the Big Dipper is about five times the distance between these two pointer stars. Do not expect to find a very bright star. Polaris, the star at the end of the handle of the Little Dipper, is about as bright as Merak.

To measure the altitude of Polaris, you can build an astrolabe like the one shown in Figure 8b. When you look at the North Star through the soda straw, the string will hang along a line that measures the star's altitude. Have a partner read the astrolabe when you have located Polaris in your straw. What is the altitude of Polaris? What is the latitude of your location?

While you are measuring the North Star's altitude, have someone help you mark a north-south line of sight along level ground. To do this, stand looking at Polaris. Direct your helper to move until he or she is directly under your sight line to Polaris. A straight line drawn from you to your helper will provide a north-south line that will be useful in the next experiment.

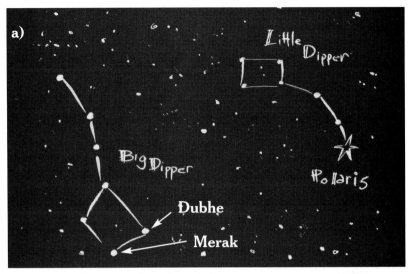

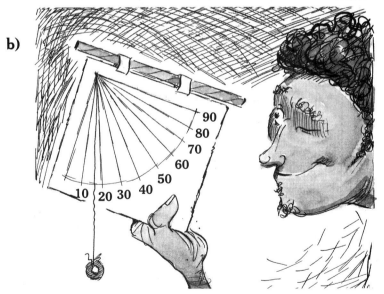

Figure 8.

a) The Big Dipper stars Merak and Dubhe form a line that points to Polaris. Five times the distance between these two stars is approximately the distance from Dubhe to Polaris.

b) An astrolobe can be made from cardboard, string, a straw, tape, a weight, and a protractor. Sight on a star through the straw. The string will mark the altitude of the star in degrees.

Science Project Ideas

- Use your astrolabe to find the angle between Polaris and Dubhe. What is the angle between Merak and Dubhe?

- If Merak and Dubhe were both ten light-years away from Earth (they aren't), what would be the distance between them in light-years and in kilometers?

Experiment 1.6

Finding Your Longitude

Materials

- ✓ accurate clock or watch
- ✓ north-south line drawn in previous experiment
- ✓ stick
- ✓ GPS (Global Positioning System) receiver (optional)

Finding your longitude is not as easy as finding your latitude. With an accurate timepiece and knowledge of the time in Greenwich, England, you can determine your approximate longitude by measuring the time of midday. Sailors used to use a sextant to take five or more sightings of the Sun beginning about 20 minutes prior to midday, and another five during the 20 minutes after midday. These readings were used to determine the exact time of midday.

You can establish midday using the north-south line you drew in the previous experiment. Place a stick vertically at the south end of your north-south line. When the stick's shadow falls on the north-south line, you know that the Sun is midway across the sky and, therefore, it is midday. Midday will probably not occur at noon. For the average time zone, it takes an hour for the Sun to move from the zone's eastern edge to its western edge. Furthermore, the time of midday for any location varies with the season.

Suppose, for example, that you find midday occurs at 12:35 P.M. If you know it is 7:00 P.M. in Greenwich, the time difference since it was midday in Greenwich is 6 hours and 25 minutes. Since every hour represents a change of 15 degrees, you know you are 96.25 degrees west of Greenwich.

$$6 \text{ hours and } 25 \text{ minutes} = 6 \, {}^{25}\!/_{60} \text{ hours} = 6.417 \text{ hours}$$

$$6.417 \text{ hr} \times 15°/\text{hr} = 96.25°$$

Your longitude is 96.25° west of Greenwich, somewhere in the midwestern United States.

Use your north-south line and a clock or watch to estimate your longitude. How closely does it agree with a value you can find on a map or globe?

Today, hikers, canoeists, and others traveling through wilderness can find their position very accurately using a GPS (Global Positioning System) receiver. These relatively inexpensive handheld receivers can pick up signals from satellites orbiting Earth.

The GPS consists of 24 NAVSTAR satellites in orbits about Earth's poles at altitudes of more than 16,000 km (10,000 mi). The satellites contain atomic clocks that transmit radio signals at very precise times. Receivers equipped with computers compare the times the signals were sent with the time they were received. With this information, the distance of the receiver from the satellites can be established, since radio signals travel at the speed of light (300,000 km/s, or 186,000 mi/s).

Because times can be measured to tenths of microseconds (0.0000001 s) or better, your position can be found to within a few meters of your true location. Your longitude and latitude are displayed on a screen.

If possible, use a GPS receiver to find your latitude and longitude. How closely do they agree with the values you found in your experiments?

Science Project Ideas

- What is the loran system of navigation and how does it work?

- How many signals need to be received from different satellites for a GPS receiver to determine your longitude and latitude?

Experiment 1.7

Does Earth Turn?

Materials

- ✓ heavy metal washer
- ✓ thread
- ✓ tape
- ✓ cabinet or table
- ✓ lazy Susan

In the previous experiment you read that the Sun moves about Earth at a rate of 15 degrees per hour. But you have probably been told that the Sun only appears to move. It is really Earth rotating from west to east that makes the Sun appear to move from east to west. Since the time of Galileo (1564–1642), astronomers were quite certain that even though the Sun,

Moon, and stars appear to move around Earth, it was really Earth that turned. But how could they be certain? There was no direct proof until 1851 when Jean Foucault (1819–1868), a French physicist, carried out an experiment to show that Earth really does rotate.

Foucault hung a 65-m-long pendulum with a 28-kg bob from the dome of the Pantheon in Paris. Foucault knew that a pendulum will maintain the plane of its swing. He reasoned that if Earth really turns, the plane of the pendulum's swing should appear to move westward as Earth rotated beneath it.

Some science museums and colleges have Foucault pendulums. If you go to such a place, you can see for yourself that Earth truly does rotate. However, you can make a simple model to show how a Foucault pendulum works. Make a pendulum from a heavy metal washer and a piece of thread. Use tape to hang the pendulum from a cabinet or table, as shown in Figure 9. Set the pendulum swinging above a lazy Susan. The center of the lazy Susan represents Earth's North Pole. Use a piece of tape to show the plane of the pendulum's swing. Slowly turn the lazy Susan from west to east (counterclockwise) to represent a rotating Earth. Notice how the plane of the pendulum's swing appears to rotate from east to west just as Foucault's pendulum did in the Pantheon.

cabinet

thread

tape to
show
pendulum
path

washer

Slowly turn
lazy Susan
eastward.

Figure 9.

In the model, the center of the lazy Susan represents Earth's
North Pole. What happens to the apparent path of the pendulum as "Earth" turns from west to east?

Experiment 1.8

Path of a Satellite

Materials

✓ globe   ✓ pencil

✓ string   ✓ a partner

✓ flat projection map of the world

You may have seen a map (on television or in a newspaper) showing the path of a satellite. Perhaps you were surprised to see an S-shaped path, as shown in Figure 10, rather than a circular or elliptical one.

Why does the path of a satellite have an S shape when seen on a flat map of the world?

To answer this question you will need a globe, a piece of string long enough to go around the globe at its equator, a flat map of the world, a pencil, and a partner. The string can be used to show the satellite's path around the globe. Begin by assuming the satellite is launched from Cape Kennedy in Florida. The string then should pass over Cape Kennedy and be so oriented that half the orbit is above the equator and half below.

Have a partner hold the string in place firmly against the globe. On the globe, note the maximum distance of the string (orbit) above the equator. Use a pencil to mark that point on the flat map of the world. Do the same for the maximum

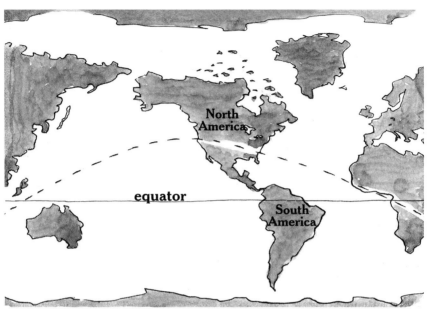

Figure 10.

The dotted line shows the path of a satellite projected on a flat map of the world.

distance below the equator. Then make an X at Cape Kennedy on the flat map of the world. Continue to note familiar points through which the string passes and transfer those points to the flat map. You will need to mark about 15 to 20 such points on the map. Once the marks have been made on the map, connect them with a smooth curved line. What does the satellite's path look like on the flat map?

Chapter 2

The Moon: Our Largest and Only Natural Satellite

Objects that move around (orbit) a planet are called satellites. There are many satellites orbiting Earth. All but one of them have been placed in orbit by humans. Rockets launched some of them into space from Earth; space shuttles already in orbit released others. Earth's only natural satellite is the Moon. Some planets, such as Jupiter, have many moons. Earth has only one.

In this chapter you will investigate the Moon by watching it and seeing how it changes with time. You may be surprised to learn that you can often see the Moon during the day as well as at night. There are also days when you can't see it at any time. You will track the Moon's path about Earth and the Sun. And you will make models to demonstrate what happens when Earth passes between the Moon and Sun, or the Moon between Earth and the Sun.

Experiment 2.1

Watching the Moon by Day and by Night

Materials

- ✓ daily newspaper with information about the Moon
- ✓ notebook
- ✓ pen or pencil

To see how the Moon changes over time, you will need to record your observations about the Moon in a notebook. A good time to begin your observations is a day or two after a new moon. When the Moon is between Earth and the Sun, it is called a new moon. A newspaper or an almanac will give the date of a new moon. You can usually find this information in the weather section of the paper. Several days after the date of a new moon, look for the Moon as the Sun sets.

You can look at the Moon as much as you want. But **never look directly at the Sun. It can cause serious damage to your eyes!**

Each time you observe the Moon, use a notebook to record the date, the time, and a drawing to show what the Moon looks like. You should also record the direction in which you find the Moon—north (N), south (S), east (E), west (W), or a direction in between, such as southwest (SW). Record, too, the altitude of the Moon above the horizon and, if possible, the distance (angle) between the Moon and the Sun.

Distances and altitudes in the sky are usually measured as angles. Sometimes the Sun and Moon appear close together in the sky. They might be less than 20 degrees apart because they lie near the same imaginary line extending from your eye into space.

The Sun and Moon are actually about 150 million km (93 million mi) apart. Since the Moon orbits Earth, its average distance from the Sun is the same as Earth's distance from the Sun. When people say the Moon is close to the Sun, they mean that the angle between the Moon and the Sun in the sky is small (see Figure 11a).

You can make good estimates of angles by using your fists. If you hold your fist at arm's length as shown in Figure 12a, it will cover approximately 10 degrees in the sky. To see that each fist really is equal to about 10 degrees, start with your fist closed and extended toward the horizon (azimuth). Go fist on fist upward, as shown in the drawing, until one arm points straight up. You will find it takes just about 9 fists to reach this point.

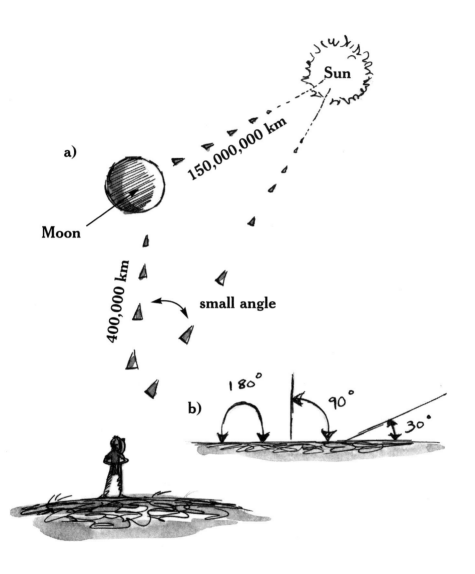

Figure 11.

a) Even though the Sun and Moon are far apart, they may appear to be close together in the sky. b) These are some of the angles between the Sun and Moon that you may measure.

Since horizontal to straight overhead (the zenith) is 90 degrees, each fist must cover about 10 degrees ($90° \div 9 = 10°$).

To find the angular distance between the Sun and the Moon, cover the Sun with one of your hands as you begin so that **you are not looking directly at the Sun.** Then find how many fists separate the Sun and Moon. Record the angle between the Sun and Moon in your notebook. A typical record for one observation in this experiment is shown in Figure 12b.

Each clear evening for the next few days, try to observe the Moon at about the time of sunset. Make the same measurements you made before and record them in your notebook. Also look for the Moon early in the morning, before sunrise, and at other times of the day and night. Record all your observations of the Moon in your notebook.

What happens to the shape of the Moon as days pass? What happens to the distance (angle) between the Moon and Sun from one sunset to the next? What happens to the Moon's location in the sky at sunset as the days pass? Is the Moon moving more to the east or to the west of the Sun as days go by? What does this tell you about the time that the Moon rises? Is it rising earlier or later each day?

About two weeks after a new moon, if it is clear, you will see a full moon. Where is the Sun when you see a full moon rising?

Keep recording data about the Moon as far into the evening as possible. Can you see the Moon the next morning when you get up?

a)

b)

Moon Data				
Appearance	Direction	Date & Time	Altitude	Sun-Moon Angle
☽	SW	11/4, 4:10 P.M.	30°	25°

Figure 12.

a) Hold your fist at arm's length, the top of your fist even with the horizon. Then go upward fist on fist until one fist is directly over your head. You will find you have gone 9 fists to cover the 90 degrees from horizontal to overhead. This means your fist at arm's length covers about 10 degrees of sky.

b) Sample data for one observation of the Moon.

Through approximately how many degrees does the Moon move in one hour? How could you estimate the distance (angle) between the Sun and Moon even if the Sun has set?

When the Moon is no longer visible at sunset, begin looking for it early in the morning, before, during, and after sunrise. What is the Moon's shape? Which side of the Moon (left or right) is now the brighter side? Is this the side nearer or farther from the Sun?

Continue your observations of the Moon for several months. You will begin to see a pattern to the Moon's motion and changing appearance. How much time passes between one full moon and the next? Does the full moon always rise in the same place (direction) on the horizon?

Science Project Ideas

- Jupiter, the largest planet in our solar system, has many moons. You can see some of them by looking through binoculars. How many can you see? How can you tell that they go around the planet?

- Do some research to find out how many moons orbit each of the planets in our solar system. Are there any planets that have no satellites?

Experiment 2.2

A Model of Moon, Earth, and Sun

Materials

- ✓ dark room
- ✓ lamp and bright lightbulb
- ✓ a partner
- ✓ a light-colored ball, about 2–4 inches in diameter (a Styrofoam ball works well), mounted on a stick or nail

Scientists often make models (theories) to explain what they observe and the data they collect. In some cases the theory can be illustrated by a physical model. In this experiment you will examine a physical model of the Moon, Earth, and Sun to see if it agrees with the data you collected in the previous experiment.

To begin, put a single bright lightbulb at one end of a dark room. The lightbulb represents the Sun. Ask a partner to stand beside you and hold a light-colored ball mounted on a stick. If the ball is made of Styrofoam, the stick can be pushed into the ball. If you can't find a Styrofoam ball, use a tennis ball mounted on a long nail. Have your partner stand to your left while you face the light, as shown in Figure 13.

In this model your head represents Earth; the light-colored ball is the Moon. Since you are facing the Sun (the light in this model), the model now represents Earth at noon when the Sun is in the middle of its path across the sky. The Moon (small

Figure 13.

This model represents Earth, Moon, and Sun.

ball) is to the east. Slowly turn your head and body toward the east (toward the Moon). Your turning represents Earth as it rotates on its axis. In your model, you are seeing the Moon rise. After you make one quarter of a turn, the Sun (lightbulb) will be on your right (west). It is sunset. The Moon is directly in front of you, so it is in the middle of the sky.

Figure 14a shows Earth (your head), Moon (ball), and Sun (lightbulb) in your model from above. You (Earth) are facing the Moon after one-quarter turn. Half the Moon is lighted, the other half is dark. The Moon is at first quarter. Have you ever seen the Moon when it looked like this? If you have, at what angle was it from the Sun?

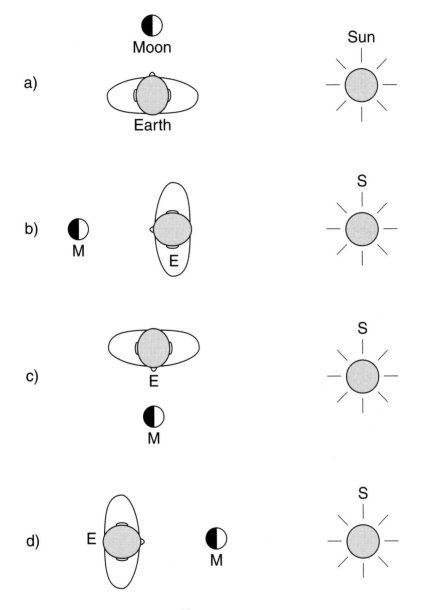

Figure 14.

The model can be used to show the position of the Moon at (a) first quarter; (b) full moon; (c) third quarter; (d) new moon.

Continue to turn slowly to your left to represent a rotating Earth. You will see the Moon set after another quarter turn. As you continue to rotate, you will see the Sun rise and move slowly across the "sky." Then you will again face the Moon.

In the next model, the Moon moves slowly around Earth. After a week (seven full rotations of Earth) the Moon has moved to a point where it is on the opposite side of Earth from the Sun. To represent this model, have your partner slowly move the Moon (ball) one quarter of the way around you while you make seven complete rotations (turns). Watch what happens to the Moon's appearance as you make these turns. When you face the Moon now (Figure 14b), it will be a full moon. (If the Moon is in the shadow of your head, have your partner raise the ball.)

During another seven turns of Earth, the Moon will move slowly to the position shown in Figure 14c. At this point, again only half the Moon you see is bright (last quarter). But it is now the other half that receives the "sunshine." After another seven turns of Earth, the Moon will lie between Earth and the Sun (Figure 14d). Since no reflected light can reach you, you will not see the Moon. It is a new moon. Of course, a room is not a perfect model of space. Some light reflected by the walls and ceiling will reach the ball. This makes the dimly lighted ball visible. In the space around the real Moon, there are no walls or ceilings to reflect light, so it cannot be seen. The lighted side faces the Sun.

Repeat the experiment once more. While you (Earth) turn about 28 times, have your partner move the Moon once around you. Then give your partner a chance to be the rotating Earth while you move the Moon.

About the Model

A good model will agree with what is found in the real world. Does the model you have just examined agree with the observations of the Moon that you made in Experiment 2.1? Did the real Moon change from a thin crescent to a half moon, then to a full moon? Did it then, after a week, appear as another half moon (with the opposite side bright)? Over the following week did it again become a crescent (but reversed), and then disappear before returning as a thin crescent near sunset?

If your answers to these questions are all yes, then your model of the Moon is a good one. According to the model, as Earth rotates on its axis, the Moon moves around Earth every 28 days (about once a month).

What is a "blue moon?" What is meant by the phrase "once in a blue moon?"

Science Project Ideas

- Although lunar satellites have photographed all sides of the Moon, only astronauts have actually seen the far side of the Moon. Design a model to show why we always see the same side of the Moon.

- You have seen a crescent moon shortly after sunset. What does that same crescent moon look like to someone in Argentina? Design a model to explain.

Experiment 2.3

The Moon's Orbit About Earth and Sun

Materials

- ✓ tape
- ✓ wrapping paper
- ✓ meterstick
- ✓ string
- ✓ a friend
- ✓ pencil or marking pen
- ✓ protractor

According to the model you examined in the previous experiment, the Moon orbits Earth in 28 days. Since Earth orbits the

Sun once a year, the Moon must also follow a path around the Sun. You might think the Moon's path about the Sun is like the one shown in Figure 15. But the actual path of the Moon is quite different.

To see what the Moon's orbit about the Sun looks like, you need to make a scale model. Earth is approximately 150,000,000 km from the Sun. The distance between the Moon and Earth is approximately 400,000 km. The distances vary a little because the orbits are not perfect circles.

You can make a scale model of part of the orbits of Earth and the Moon about the Sun. In this model we will let one centimeter represent one million kilometers. Therefore, Earth's orbit will have a radius of 150 cm (1.5 m). To draw part of this orbit, you will need to tape together some large

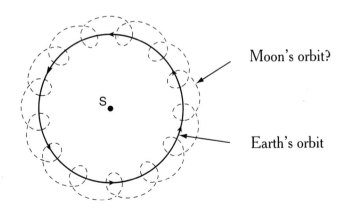

Figure 15.

Is this diagram a good representation of the Moon's path around the Sun?

sheets of wrapping paper. The final sheet of paper should be a square about 1.6 m (5 ft 3 in) on a side.

Let the lower left-hand corner of the paper represent the position of the Sun. Cut a piece of string a little longer than 1.5 m. Have a friend hold one end of the string on the lower left-hand corner of the paper. Hold a pencil or marking pen against the string at a point 150 cm from the end your friend is holding. Using the string as a radius, draw the representation of Earth's orbit as shown in Figure 16.

Next, using a protractor and the meterstick, draw radii from the Sun to Earth at 0 degrees, 30 degrees, 60 degrees, and 90 degrees. Since Earth travels 360 degrees around the Sun in one year, it will travel about 30 degrees (360 ÷ 12) in one month. Start with Earth (E) on the starting radius at 0 degrees and the Moon at a new moon position, as shown. Since the Moon (M) is about 400,000 km from Earth, it will be 4 mm (0.4 cm) closer to the Sun than Earth. This distance is too small to show on the scale drawing in Figure 16, so the distances between Moon and Earth are larger than they should be.

Mark Earth's position at one-week intervals as shown. Remember: The Moon moves one quarter of the way around Earth every seven days. So, after seven days from the new moon, the Moon has traveled counterclockwise around Earth to the first quarter moon. The Moon will move to positions representing new moon (start), first quarter, full moon, third quarter, new moon, and so on.

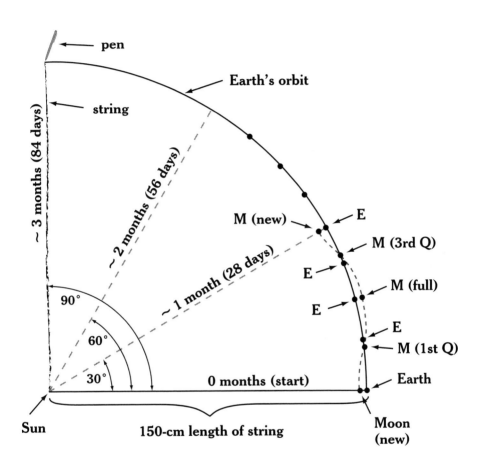

Figure 16.

Draw one quarter of Earth's orbit to a scale of 1 cm = 150,000,000 km. Then draw the Moon's orbit about the Sun as a dotted line. The Moon on this scale will be 0.4 cm from Earth. The distance is somewhat exaggerated in this drawing.

Mark Earth's and Moon's position at weekly intervals for the three-month section of Earth's orbit you have drawn. Then connect the Moon's successive positions with a dotted line. You now have a good representation of one quarter of the Moon's orbit about the Sun. Does it look like the orbital path shown in Figure 15?

Science Project Ideas

- Knowing the distance between Earth and the Moon, design and carry out an experiment to measure the diameter of the Moon.

- Knowing the distance between Earth and the Sun, design and carry out an experiment to measure the diameter of the Sun. **Remember: Never look directly at the Sun.**

Experiment 2.4

An Eclipse of the Moon

Materials

✓ scissors

✓ soda straw

✓ coin

✓ white file card

✓ frosted lightbulb, socket, and electrical outlet

✓ dark room

✓ Styrofoam or clay balls 5 cm (2 in) and 1.2–1.3 cm (0.5 in) in diameter

✓ stick 1.5 m (5 ft) long

✓ 2 small finishing nails

✓ tape

As you saw in Experiment 1.3, a sphere always casts a round shadow. Occasionally, at the time of a full moon, Earth, Moon, and Sun lie along a line on the same plane, as shown in Figure 17a. Like any object in sunlight, Earth casts a shadow. We are in Earth's shadow every night after sunset. When the full moon enters that shadow, a lunar eclipse occurs.

Shadows vary in darkness. To see the difference in darkness, use scissors to make a small slit in the top of a soda straw. Insert a coin in the slit. The straw can serve as a handle. Hold a white file card several feet from a glowing frosted lightbulb in an otherwise dark room. Bring the coin near the card so that you see its dark shadow (umbra) on the paper. Now slowly move the coin away from the card. You will see the dark umbra grow smaller, while a fuzzy lighter shadow, the penumbra,

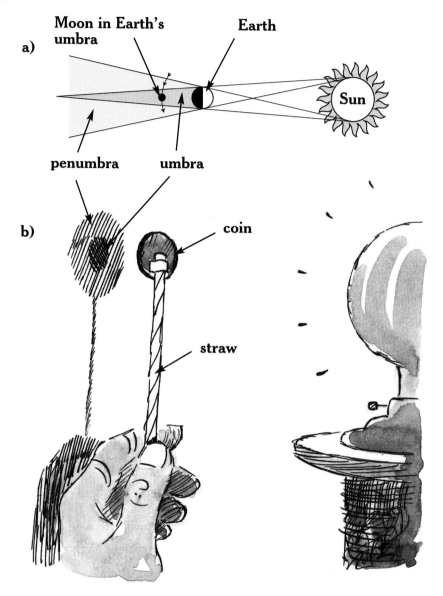

Figure 17.

a) Earth casts a shadow. When the Moon enters Earth's shadow, a lunar eclipse occurs. b) A coin casts a shadow. The dark part of the shadow is the umbra. No light from the bulb reaches the umbra. The lighter part of the shadow is the penumbra. Some light reaches the penumbra.

grows larger (see Figure 17b). Save the coin and straw for the next experiment.

As Figure 17a reveals, Earth's shadow has an umbra and a penumbra. If you examine the drawing carefully, you can see that some light from the Sun reaches the penumbra. No direct sunlight reaches the umbra. The Moon darkens as it enters Earth's penumbra and becomes much darker if it reaches the umbra. The darkened Moon has a copper color, but it doesn't disappear. The atmosphere bends a little of the Sun's light around Earth so that some sunlight reaches the Moon. Therefore, our view of the Moon is never totally blocked by Earth's shadow, even when the Moon lies within the dark umbra of Earth's shadow.

You can make a scale model of a lunar eclipse. To do so you will need a Styrofoam or clay ball 5 cm (2 in) in diameter and another with a diameter of 1.2–1.3 cm (0.5 in). You will also need a stick 1.5 m (5 ft) long and two small finishing nails, one taped to each end of the stick, as shown in Figure 18. The large ball represents Earth. The small ball represents the Moon, which has a diameter that is a bit more than one-quarter Earth's diameter. The centers of Earth and Moon are about 30 Earth-diameters apart. A stick 1.5 m (5 ft) long will separate the model Earth and Moon by just about the distance needed for a scale model.

The real Sun can serve as the Sun in this model. It is much too far away to fit the scale. However, light rays reaching Earth from the Sun are almost parallel, so the Sun's size and distance aren't important for this model.

Hold the stick so that Earth is closest to the Sun, as shown in Figure 18. Tip and turn the stick until Sun, Earth, and Moon are in line. When they are, Earth's shadow will fall on the Moon. To see the Moon move into and out of Earth's shadow, turn the stick slightly on a horizontal plane, using Earth as the axis.

How much do you have to tilt the stick to move the Moon out of Earth's shadow? Why do you think an eclipse does not occur at the time of every full moon?

Save your model for the next experiment.

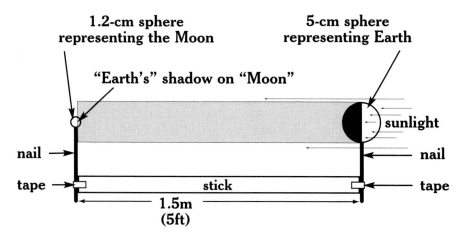

Figure 18.

Two spheres 1.5 meters (5 feet) apart can be used to make a scale model of Earth and the Moon. What conditions are needed to produce a lunar eclipse using this model?

Science Project Idea

Look closely at the shadow of a flagpole or telephone pole. Notice that the shadow near the base of the pole is dark like an umbra. Farther out, the shadow shows a penumbra outside the umbra. If the shadow is long, its end may be fuzzy and light and have no umbra. How can you explain such a shadow? Does your shadow have a similar appearance?

Experiment 2.5

An Eclipse of the Sun

Materials

✓ model you used in the previous experiment

✓ frosted incandescent lightbulb and socket

✓ coin mounted on a soda straw used in the previous experiment

✓ white file card or a white wall

Turn the model you used in the previous experiment so that the Moon is closer than the Earth to the Sun. Move the stick until the Moon's shadow falls on Earth. You now have a model of a solar eclipse. A solar eclipse occurs when the Moon's shadow falls on Earth. During a solar eclipse, the

Sun, or part of it, is hidden by the Moon. Because the Moon is so small, its shadow covers only part of Earth. The Moon's shadow, like Earth's (and yours), has a dark portion (umbra) and a fuzzy portion (penumbra). As Figure 19a shows, the umbra touches only a tiny part of Earth's surface, if any. Only a small part of Earth will be covered by the darkest part of the Moon's shadow (the umbra), where all of the Sun's light is blocked by the Moon. As Earth, Sun, and Moon move, the Moon's umbra traces a narrow path across Earth's surface. The width of this shadow never exceeds 274 km (170 mi). Sometimes only the penumbra reaches Earth (see Figure 19b). When that happens, part of the Sun is always visible during the eclipse.

You can make another model of a solar eclipse that will show you what the Sun looks like during a total and a partial solar eclipse. An ordinary lighted frosted incandescent light-bulb can represent the Sun. Use the coin mounted on the soda straw that you used in the previous experiment to represent the Moon.

Stand several feet from the glowing lightbulb. Hold the coin in front of one eye and close your other eye. Move the coin back and forth until it covers all of the lightbulb. The entire bulb will disappear when the umbra of the coin's shadow falls on the pupil of your eye. The entire view of the bulb will be blocked from your eye. The coin (Moon) has totally eclipsed the bulb (Sun). Move the coin slightly to the

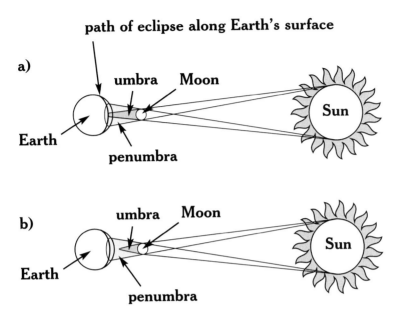

path of eclipse along Earth's surface

a)

umbra   Moon

Earth

Sun

penumbra

b)

umbra   Moon

Earth

Sun

penumbra

Figure 19.

a) A solar eclipse occurs when the Moon's shadow falls on Earth. If the umbra reaches Earth's surface, people within the umbra will see a total solar eclipse. That is, the Sun will be completely blocked by the Moon. Within the penumbra, there will be a partial eclipse. Only part of the Sun will be blocked from view. b) If the umbra does not reach Earth's surface, there will not be a total eclipse anywhere on Earth's surface.

side, and part of the bulb becomes visible. Part of your eye is in the coin's umbra and part is in its penumbra. In the same way, the Moon, during a solar eclipse, casts a shadow on Earth. Where the shadow falls, it blocks from view part or all of the Sun. **Do not do this experiment outdoors using the real Sun!**

Move the coin closer to your eye. Does it block out more or less of the bulb? Slowly move the coin farther from your eye. Does the coin block out more or less of the bulb as you move it away? Hold the coin far enough away so that it blocks the center part of the lightbulb but leaves a ring of light around the edge. This is what happens during what is called an annular solar eclipse. In an annular eclipse, a thin ring of light is still visible all around the edge of the Sun because the umbra part of the Moon's shadow does not reach Earth's surface.

When the coin blocks out the top, bottom, or one side of the lightbulb, you have what happens during a partial eclipse, when you are in the penumbra portion of the Moon's shadow. Because the Moon's umbra never stretches more than 274 km across Earth's surface, you are more likely to see a partial eclipse than a total eclipse.

Replace your eye with a white file card or a white wall to represent Earth's surface. Let the coin's shadow fall on the card or wall. You have an astronaut's view of Earth's surface during an eclipse. Can you find the region where there is a total eclipse? A partial eclipse? Can you move the coin so that no part of the umbra reaches the card or wall? What kind of an eclipse does this represent?

If you have an opportunity to view a solar eclipse, **never look at the Sun!** Even during an eclipse, the Sun is so bright it can severely damage your eyes. One way to view a solar eclipse is to make a pinhole image of the Sun. Make a pinhole in one side of a large cardboard box. Turn the box so that the pinhole faces the Sun. With your back to the Sun, place the box over your head. You can view the Sun's image on a sheet of white paper taped to the side of the box opposite the pinhole. Sunlight entering the box through the pinhole will form an image on the screen.

Look under a leafy tree during an eclipse. You will see many pinhole images of the eclipsed Sun.

Science Project Ideas

- Use a pinhole image of the Sun and the known distance to the Sun (150,000,000 km) to measure the Sun's diameter. **Remember: Never look directly at the Sun!**

- Mercury and Venus sometimes come between the Sun and Earth. Why don't they cause eclipses of the Sun?

Chapter 3

Our Changing Earth

Most of us think of Earth as one of the few unchanging things in our lives. But if we lived for centuries or millennia instead of years, we would see continents move and mountains rise and disappear. We also tend to think that water, which makes life on Earth possible, is found in oceans, lakes, and ponds. But there are huge amounts of water in aquifers under the ground we walk on. Wells are drilled to reach that water. Underground water is often the sole source for entire communities.

Experiment 3.1

Today's Continents and Yesterday's Pangaea

Materials

✓ tracing paper   ✓ pencil

✓ globe or large map   ✓ scissors
of the world

Geologists tell us that Earth's continents rest on plates about 80 to 160 km (50 to 100 mi) thick. These plates are moving slowly as a result of forces beneath Earth's crust. About 200 million years ago, the continents were all together in a single landmass or continent called Pangaea. Since that time, movement of the plates has divided the continents and separated them by oceans and seas. Some remain connected by narrow strips of land.

If all the continents were once part of Pangaea, we might expect them to fit together like pieces of a jigsaw puzzle. Of course, the fits may not be perfect, because ocean levels have changed and continental edges have eroded over time.

To see how well the continents fit together, you can cut out the shape of each continent from construction paper. To do this, place a sheet of tracing paper over North America on a globe or large map of the world. Using a pencil, trace the outline of the continent on the paper. Use scissors to cut out the continent's shape. Then use the tracing paper as a template to cut the continent's shape from construction paper.

Repeat this process for each continent. How well do the shapes of the continents fit together? Based on your observations, which continents do you think were the last to separate from one another? Which do you think were the first to separate? What makes you think so?

Experiment 3.2

Mountains and Erosion

Materials

- ✓ **an adult**
- ✓ 2 pads of paper
- ✓ dry bar of soap
- ✓ balance for weighing
- ✓ sink and faucet
- ✓ notebook and pen or pencil
- ✓ 2 long, narrow cardboard boxes, such as candy boxes
- ✓ aluminum foil
- ✓ nail
- ✓ soil
- ✓ grass seed
- ✓ water
- ✓ warm, well-lighted area
- ✓ books or blocks of wood
- ✓ plastic containers
- ✓ watering can
- ✓ 2 sheets of cardboard
- ✓ sand
- ✓ sandbox about 60 cm (2 ft) x 150 cm (5 ft)
- ✓ outdoor electrical outlet or extension cord
- ✓ glue
- ✓ wooden coffee stirrers or craft sticks
- ✓ fan, variable speed if available

Earth's surface is constantly changing, but the changes are slow to occur. The mountains we see today arose when the plates on which continents rest collided.

To see how the collision of these plates, called tectonic plates, can give rise to mountains, you will need two pads of paper. Carefully push the pads together as shown in Figure 20. One of two things may happen. In one case (a), the ends of both pads rise. In the other (b), one pad slides under the second, pushing it higher. In either case, you can see how when plates collide, the land rises, forming mountains.

While continents slowly change position, their surfaces change as well because of erosion. Although erosion is generally

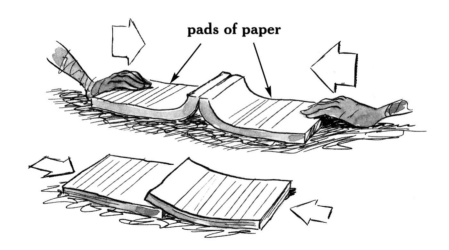

pads of paper

Figure 20.

Mountains form when the plates covering Earth collide as they are moved by forces deep beneath Earth's surface. The paper pads represent two plates that are being pushed together.

a slow process, over millions of years it can wear away mountains. But erosion can also cause mountains to grow taller. Erosion makes the mountains lighter. This causes the mountains, which float on the denser mantle beneath the crust, to rise. In much the same way, a heavy cargo ship floats higher in the water when its cargo is removed.

Why might the collision of Earth's plates cause earthquakes?

Erosion is not limited to mountains, but wherever it occurs, it is usually a slow process. Therefore, it is best to begin with an artificial example that will accelerate the process. You can do this by weighing a dry bar of soap. Record the weight and the time. Then put the soap in a sink and let a steady drip (not a stream) from a faucet fall on the center of the soap. Do this just before your family goes to bed so that water can drip on the soap all night.

The next morning, count the number of drops of water that are hitting the soap each minute. Record that number and the time. Then remove the bar of soap and let it dry.

When the soap is dry, reweigh it. How much soap eroded away? How many drops of water were required to produce the erosion? What is the rate of erosion in grams of soap per hour? What is the rate of erosion in grams of soap per liter of water? (It takes approximately 20,000 drops of water to fill a one-liter flask.)

Soil Erosion

Line two long, narrow, cardboard boxes, such as candy boxes, with aluminum foil. Use a nail to punch holes in one end of each box, as shown in Figure 21a. Add equal amounts of soil to each box. Sprinkle grass seed over the soil in one box and gently work the seeds into the top of the soil. Sprinkle the soil in both boxes with water and keep the soil in both boxes moist. Place the boxes in a warm, well-lighted area.

When the grass is growing well, use books or blocks of wood to tilt both trays at the same angle, as shown in Figure 21b. Place a plastic container under the lower end of each box. Using a watering can, sprinkle a quart of water over each box of soil. Eroded soil will collect in the containers. If very little erosion occurs, sprinkle another quart or two of water onto each box. In which soil, seeded or unseeded, is the erosion greater? Can you explain why? Would you expect more erosion on a grassy or a soil-covered slope?

Repeat the experiment, but this time fill both boxes with the same amount of loose, unseeded soil. Tilt one box so that its upper end is about twice as high as the other box's. In which box is there more erosion? Can you explain why? Would you expect more erosion to occur on steep mountains or on rolling hills that have a gentle slope? What is the effect of gravity on erosion?

Can you find evidence of soil erosion near your home? If you can, what might be done to reduce the erosion?

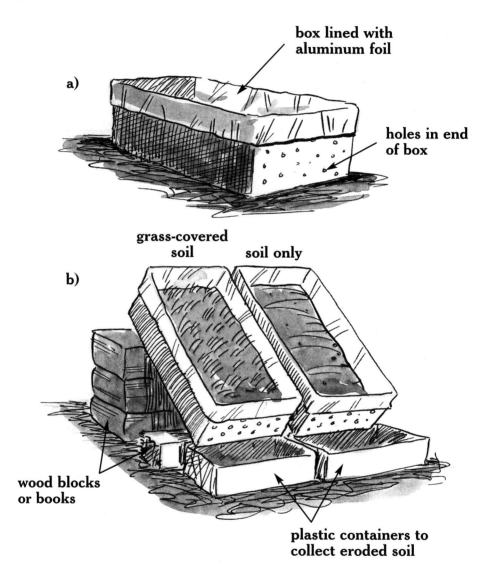

a) box lined with aluminum foil

holes in end of box

grass-covered soil

soil only

b)

wood blocks or books

plastic containers to collect eroded soil

Figure 21.

a) Holes are made in one end of each box to allow eroded soil to exit. b) Erosion from tilted boxes containing plain and grass-covered soil can be compared.

Erosion Due to Wind

To see how wind can cause erosion, place two sheets of cardboard on level ground outdoors. Place a small pile of sand on each sheet. Sprinkle water on one pile until the sand is wet. Next, blow across both piles of sand. What do you observe? Explain how a severe drought can contribute to soil erosion.

Sand particles and snowflakes can be carried long distances by wind. You may have seen snow fences along highways and similar fences on ocean beaches. The fences are designed to reduce the wind's speed, causing wind-borne particles to fall. In this way, snow is kept off roads and sand is prevented from blowing off beaches onto nearby land or highways. To see how these fences trap sand particles, you will need an outdoor sandbox. The box should be about 60 cm (2 ft) × 150 cm (5 ft) and contain dry sand about 5 cm (2 in) deep. Place the box near an outdoor electrical outlet or have **an adult** connect an extension cord to an indoor outlet.

Make a miniature fence by gluing together wooden coffee stirrers or craft sticks as shown in Figure 22a. Leave about 5 cm between the centers of the vertical sticks. Bury the lower end of the fence near one end of the box. At the other end, use a fan to blow sand against the fence (see Figure 22b). **Stay behind the fan so that sand does not blow into your eyes.** Turn on the fan for about 30 seconds. Turn off the fan and look for any evidence of sand accumulating near the fence. Repeat the process several times, if necessary, until you see evidence of sand buildup around the fence. Where do sand dunes form?

Next, add more slats to the fence so that the sticks or stirrers are only about half as far apart. How does reducing the distance between the slats affect the buildup of sand?

What happens if a solid fence is used?

If your fan has variable speeds, investigate the effect of wind velocity on the fence's ability to accumulate sand.

a)
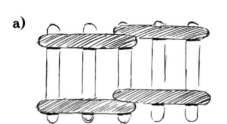

Will two fences, one behind the other, work better than a single fence? How about V-shaped fences?

b)

sand

Figure 22.

a) A model snow fence made by gluing together coffee stirrers or craft sticks. b) An experiment to test the effect of fences on wind erosion.

Science Project Ideas

- Design and build a seismograph that can detect earthquakes.

- Develop a model to show how the collision of tectonic plates can cause volcanic eruptions.

- Design and conduct an experiment to find out how the erosion of soap is affected by the speed at which the water drops strike the soap.

- Design and conduct an experiment to find out how the erosion of sand and clay soils compare.

- Demonstrate how many farmers reduce the erosion of soil from their fields.

- Find out how severe drought caused the erosion of farmland in the United States during the 1930s.

Experiment 3.3

Glacial Erosion and Melting

Materials

- ✓ ice cubes
- ✓ sand
- ✓ bar of soap
- ✓ tray
- ✓ paper towel
- ✓ sunny window
- ✓ aluminum foil
- ✓ dry soil
- ✓ ground black pepper
- ✓ dry leaves
- ✓ lampblack, powdered charcoal, bone black, charcoal, or pencil lead (graphite)
- ✓ 2 identical thermometers (⁻10°C–110°C)
- ✓ black and white construction paper
- ✓ rubber bands
- ✓ sunlight
- ✓ clock or watch
- ✓ natural winter ice

Twenty thousand years ago much of North America was covered by a glacier, a layer of ice hundreds of feet thick. Under its own weight, the glacier advanced, carving the earth beneath its surface. To see how a glacier erodes the earth over which it moves, place an ice cube on some sand. Then rub the sandy side of the ice cube over a bar of soap. What does the sand under the ice do to the soap?

Again, place the ice cube on the sand. This time let the ice cube rest on the soap and melt, like a receding glacier. What is left after the ice melts? You have created a miniature moraine.

Although much less extensive than during the ice ages, glaciers still exist. During droughts, airplanes are sometimes used to spray lampblack (powdered carbon) over a glacier. To see why, place several identical ice cubes on a tray lined with a paper towel. Put the tray near a window where sunlight will fall on the ice cubes. Cover each ice cube with a different material. You might use aluminum foil, dry soil, black pepper, and bits of dry leaves. If you have powdered carbon (lampblack, powdered charcoal, or bone black), use one or more of them. If you do not have any carbon, you can make some by scraping a piece of charcoal or the end of a pencil that has thick, black lead (graphite). One ice cube should be left uncovered to serve as a control. Which ice cube melts fastest?

To see why some ice cubes melted faster than others, you will need two identical thermometers. Wrap the bulb end of one thermometer with black construction paper. Wrap the second thermometer with white construction paper. Rubber bands can be used to hold the paper in place, as shown in Figure 23. Set both thermometers side by side in sunlight. After 15 minutes, compare the temperatures. What do you find? How does the color of the paper affect its ability to absorb solar energy?

Sprinkle one area of a patch of natural winter ice with powdered charcoal or dark soil. How do you think the darkened area of ice will compare with the surrounding ice after several hours in the Sun? Was your prediction correct?

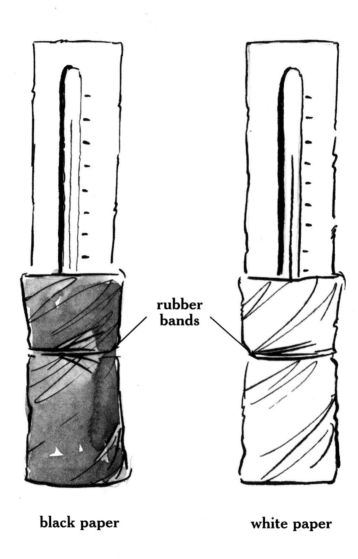

black paper   white paper

Figure 23.
Does color affect the absorption of solar energy?

Experiment 3.4

Sun, Sand, Soil, and Water

Materials

- ✓ **an adult**
- ✓ 3 identical aluminum cans
- ✓ balance for weighing
- ✓ garden soil
- ✓ water
- ✓ sand
- ✓ 3 thermometers (⁻10°C–110°C)
- ✓ sheet of cardboard
- ✓ sunny place
- ✓ black cloth
- ✓ clock or watch
- ✓ oven
- ✓ oven mitts
- ✓ hot pads

Earth's surface is covered with water and solid matter such as rocks, soil, and plants. Were it not for the vast amounts of water on Earth, the planet would be too hot to support life. This experiment will help you see how water keeps Earth at moderate temperatures.

You will need to establish conditions that will cause different substances to receive the same amount of light and, therefore, the same amount of heat. To do this, obtain three empty identical aluminum cans. Place one can on a balance and add 200 g of garden soil to the can. Pour an equal weight of water into a second can, and an equal weight of sand into a third can. Put a thermometer in each can. If their temperatures are not very nearly the same, leave them in a room until they are. Record the temperature in each can. Then put the cans on a sheet of cardboard in a sunny place. Next, cover the cans evenly with a black cloth so that light falling onto the cloth will warm all the cans.

Record the temperature in each can at 15-minute intervals for at least two hours. Which material warms fastest? Which substance—sand, garden soil, or water—shows the greatest capacity for absorbing heat; that is, which substance requires the greatest amount of heat to raise its temperature one degree?

Next, remove the thermometer and have **an adult** place the cans in a warm oven (120°F). When soil, sand, and water are all at the same temperature, use oven mitts to remove all the cans and place them on hot pads in a cool place out of the sunlight. Again, record the temperature in each container at 15-minute intervals for two hours. Predict the substance—water, soil, or sand—that will cool slowest. Was your prediction correct? Why do you think one substance cools more slowly than the others? How does water help to keep Earth's temperature at a moderate level?

Science Project Ideas

- If possible, spend a warm day at a beach by the ocean or a large lake. By midday you will probably notice that there is an onshore breeze—a wind that blows from water toward land. Explain the cause of the onshore breeze. Early the next morning, there will probably be an offshore breeze. Why?

- Look at Table 1 on page 82. Explain why the average summer and winter temperatures of cities near an ocean differ so much less than those of cities located inland, even though they may receive about the same amount of sunshine.

Table 1.

AVERAGE SUMMER AND WINTER TEMPERATURES
IN SIX U.S. CITIES

City	Average January temperature (°F)	Percent of possible January sunshine	Average July temperature (°F)	Percent of possible July sunshine
San Francisco, CA	50.7	56	61.8	66
St. Louis, MO	28.8	52	78.9	69
Portland, ME	21.5	56	68.1	63
Fargo, ND	4.3	50	70.6	72
Seattle, WA	40.6	25	65.3	65
Spokane, WA	27.0	30	69.0	70

Experiment 3.5

Aquifers: Water Beneath the Ground

Materials

- ✓ clay
- ✓ fine gravel or sand
- ✓ aquarium, plastic shoe box, or large glass bowl
- ✓ food coloring
- ✓ water
- ✓ watering can

What happens to rain that falls to the ground? Some of it evaporates quickly into the atmosphere or runs off into streams and rivers that flow into ponds, lakes, and oceans. Some is absorbed by plants. The rest seeps into the ground, collecting as groundwater—the source of spring and well water.

Under the action of gravity, groundwater permeates (soaks) downward through the soil until it reaches a level of saturation; that is, until water fills all the spaces between soil and rock particles. The level dividing saturated from unsaturated soil is called the water table. The water table is the upper level of an aquifer. An aquifer is soil or rocks that can store large amounts of water between their particles. Sometimes the water table is higher than the ground, creating a pond, lake, or swamp.

You can make a model aquifer. To do so you will need clay, fine gravel or sand, and an aquarium, clear plastic shoe box, or large clear bowl.

First, cover the bottom of the clear vessel with a somewhat irregular layer of clay. The clay represents an impermeable layer of bedrock beneath the soil. Then add a layer of sand. Use the sand to form model hills, valleys, and deep wells. The shallowest sand should have a depth of at least a centimeter above the "bedrock."

Sprinkle colored water from a watering can onto the sand. Stop frequently to observe how the water seeps into the soil. Where the soil and underlying clay meet, the clear wall should provide a good cross-sectional view of the soil.

Observe the formation of the water table. As more water is added and the water table rises, observe the formation of "ponds." To see how these might dry up during a drought, watch what happens if no water is added for several days. Then add more water and notice the rising level of the "aquifer."

Use your model to show how a pond can be created by digging into soil.

Science Project Ideas

- Aquifers are sometimes stacked like plates, one above the other. Can you build a model that has two aquifers, one above the other?

- What is an artesian well? Can you create a model of such a well?

- What might cause water to move in an aquifer? How can you use your model to illustrate such movement?

Experiment 3.6

Reaching the Aquifer: Permeability

Materials

- ✓ nail
- ✓ paper cups
- ✓ sand, gravel, clay, and garden soil
- ✓ wooden coffee stirrers or small sticks
- ✓ clear plastic or glass jars
- ✓ measuring cup

For rain water to reach the aquifer, it must permeate (soak through) the soil above the water table. How rapidly it does this depends on the soil's permeability. You can test the permeability of different soils. To do so, use a nail to punch a hole in the bottom of four paper cups. Fill the cups about two thirds of the way with different soils. Put sand in one, gravel in another, clay in a third, and garden soil in a fourth. Support the cups on wooden coffee stirrers or small sticks above clear plastic or glass jars, as shown in Figure 24. Pour half a cup of water onto each type of soil. Through which soil does the water move fastest? Which type of soil retains the most water?

You may have noticed gas bubbles as you watched the water seep into the soils. What do you think the gas is and where do you think it came from?

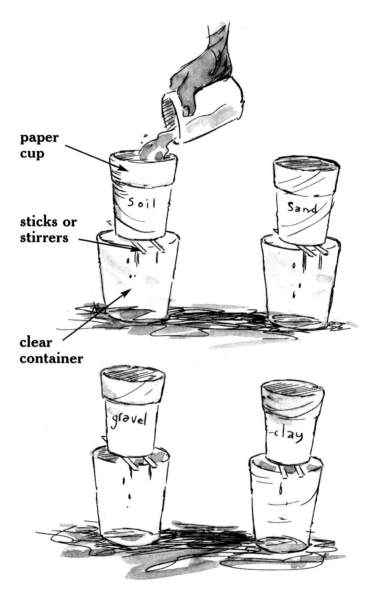

paper cup

sticks or stirrers

clear container

Figure 24.

These drawings show an experiment to test soils for permeability.

Experiment 3.7

Ocean Water: Earth's Biggest Cover

Materials

- ✓ tap water
- ✓ seawater from an ocean or kosher salt mixed with water
- ✓ 100-mL graduated cylinder
- ✓ balance for weighing
- ✓ 2 clear plastic vials
- ✓ food coloring
- ✓ eyedropper
- ✓ paper clips
- ✓ 3 insulated wires with alligator clips
- ✓ 6-volt dry-cell battery
- ✓ flashlight bulb

More than two thirds of Earth's surface is covered by ocean water, with depths as great as 11,000 m (36,000 ft or 6.8 mi). Earth's abundance of water is believed to have come from several sources. These sources include rocks that came together as Earth formed, icy comets and meteorites that collided with Earth, and the rocks in Earth's mantle that are constantly emerging through the bottom of the oceans.

Ocean water differs from the water found in lakes and ponds because it contains salts. The primary salt dissolved in seawater is sodium chloride, the salt you put on food. The concentration of salt in seawater is 3.5 percent.

If you live near an ocean, collect some seawater and bring it home. If you do not live near an ocean, you can make some seawater. Add about 3.5 g (a teaspoonful) of kosher salt to 100 mL of water and stir until the salt dissolves.

To see how seawater differs from the water we drink, you can do some tests.

The Taste Test

First place a drop of tap water and then a drop of seawater on your tongue. How do they differ in taste? **Do not drink more than a drop.**

The Density Test

Does seawater differ from drinking water in density? Density is defined as the mass or weight of a substance divided by its volume. One way to compare the densities of two substances is to weigh equal volumes of the two. You could do this by weighing 100 mL of tap water and then 100 mL of seawater. How do their densities compare?

If you are only interested in seeing if the densities differ, there is a simpler way to test. It is the method you used in Experiment 1.2. Fill one clear vial with tap water. Fill the other with seawater. Add a drop or two of food coloring to the seawater so that you can identify it. Use an eyedropper to remove some of the colored seawater from its vial. Place the end of the eyedropper below the surface of the clear tap water in the other vial. Slowly squeeze the bulb of the eyedropper so that a small amount of colored seawater enters the tap water. What happens to the seawater? Does it sink or float in the tap water? What does this tell you about the density of seawater as compared with drinking water?

Can you make two distinct liquid layers, a colored and a clear, in the vial?

Next, repeat the experiment, but this time add food coloring to the tap water. What happens when you carefully squeeze a drop of colored tap water into the middle of the vial of clear seawater? Does it rise or sink? Does the result confirm what you observed before about the comparative density of tap water and seawater?

The Conductivity Test

Some substances, such as copper, are good conductors of electricity. Other substances, such as glass, are not. To test tap water and seawater for electrical conductivity, fill a clear vial with tap water. Slide two paper clips over the edge of the vial as shown in Figure 25. Half of each paper clip should be inside the vial. Use three insulated wires with alligator clips to connect the paper clips to a 6-volt dry-cell battery and a flashlight bulb (see Figure 25). Does the bulb light?

Empty the vial and fill it with seawater. Then repeat the experiment. Does seawater conduct electricity? How can you tell?

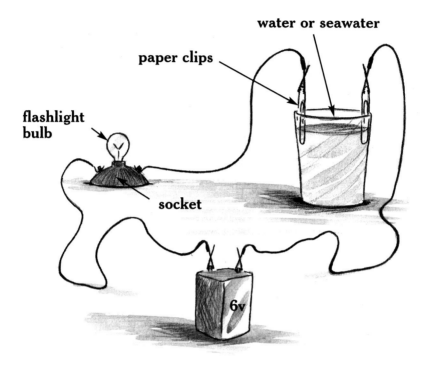

Figure 25.

Will tap water conduct electricity? Will seawater?

Science Project Idea

Design and carry out an experiment that will allow you to separate the dissolved salts in seawater from the water. What practical use would this process have?

Chapter 4

Keeping Earth Healthy

E arth is the only planet we know to have living organisms. Life on Earth is possible because its air contains the oxygen we breathe, and its soil and oceans contain the water we drink. Of course, we can't drink seawater, but most of the water in rain comes from water that evaporated from the oceans. To preserve the air we breathe and the water we drink, we must avoid polluting them with harmful substances. Unless we do, Earth will become unhealthy for life. Some parts of it already are!

Since Earth's resources are limited, it makes sense to use things again and again rather than throwing them away. This process, known as recycling, is required in many communities.

Experiment 4.1

Sand as a Filter for Aquifers

Materials

- ✓ nail
- ✓ 2 Styrofoam cups
- ✓ coffee filter
- ✓ 100-mL graduated cylinder
- ✓ clean sand
- ✓ marking pen
- ✓ 2 clear jars
- ✓ wooden coffee stirrers or craft sticks
- ✓ muddy water
- ✓ cold liquid coffee

Can sand act as a filter and remove particles and chemicals that may be washed into it?

To find out, use a nail to punch a hole in the center of the bottom of two Styrofoam cups. Place a piece of a coffee filter over the holes in the bottoms of the cups. Then pour 100 mL of sand into each cup. (The filter will prevent the sand from leaking through the hole.) Label one cup *muddy water*. Label the other cup *coffee*. Place each cup on a clear jar as shown in Figure 26. Use wooden coffee stirrers or craft sticks to support the cups.

Figure 26.

Will sand remove small particles, such as mud, from water? Will it remove a chemical such as coffee?

Pour muddy water into the appropriate cup until the cup is full. Pour cold liquid coffee into the other cup until the cup is full.

Examine the liquid that drains out the bottom of both cups. Does the sand remove the mud particles from the muddy water? Does it remove the color from coffee? How can you check to be sure it was the sand that did the filtering and not the coffee filter?

Science Project Ideas

- Design and carry out experiments to determine whether or not the size of soil particles affects its ability to filter particles that enter the soil. For instance, is fine sand a better filter than gravel?

- Design and carry out experiments to determine whether or not the size of soil particles affects the amount of water needed to saturate the soil.

- Design and carry out experiments to determine whether or not the size of soil particles affects the amount of water that the soil can retain.

Experiment 4.2

Model of a Polluted Aquifer

Materials

- ✓ sink or an outdoor area
- ✓ clean, dry gravel
- ✓ clear plastic vial
- ✓ long eyedropper
- ✓ water
- ✓ scissors
- ✓ large-diameter soda straw or 2 regular soda straws and tape
- ✓ pencil
- ✓ food coloring

Do this experiment outdoors or in a sink.

As you saw in the previous experiment, sand acts as a filter to remove solid contaminants from water that percolates through the ground into the aquifer. (Other soils will serve as filters as well.) However, soil does not filter out chemicals that dissolve in the groundwater or percolate through it.

To see how chemicals can pollute an aquifer, add clean, dry gravel to a clear plastic vial until it is about three-fourths full. The gravel represents the ground in your model. Next, fill an eyedropper with water. Use the eyedropper to "rain" on the ground in the vial. Watch the water percolate between the soil particles as you continue to add rain to the ground. Continue adding rain until the ground is saturated and a pond forms above the gravel.

Using scissors, cut a soda straw with a large diameter so that its length is the same as the height of the vial. If you can't find a straw with a large diameter, cut two ordinary straws in the same way, then cut them lengthwise and tape them together to make a straw with a bigger diameter. The straw's diameter needs to be large enough to allow the eyedropper to fit into it. Use a pencil to "drill" a well. Then use the straw to make a casing for the well as shown in Figure 27. The eyedropper can be used to pump water from your miniature aquifer. What happens to the pond as water is pumped out of the aquifer? Can you explain what happened to the pond?

Use a drop or two of food coloring to add a pollutant to the ground at a point away from the well. (The food

Figure 27.

This model of an aquifer uses gravel to represent the ground, a straw to represent a well drilled into the aquifer, and an eyedropper to pump water from the aquifer through the well. A drop or two of food coloring can represent a pollutant, such as a gasoline spill.

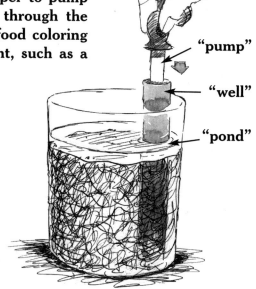

"pump"

"well"

"pond"

coloring might represent a gasoline spill that has contaminated the soil.) Add more rain to the ground. What happens to the pollution as rain enters the aquifer? Now pump more water from the aquifer. Do you see the pollutant moving toward the well?

Continue to add rain and pump water from the aquifer. Can you detect pollution in the well water?

One way to clean up a polluted aquifer is to repeatedly pump water from the aquifer, filter it, and return it to the aquifer. Rain and filtered water will gradually dilute the pollution until the water is again safe to drink. Without filtering, how many pumpings and "rainstorms" are required to clean up your model aquifer?

Experiment 4.3

Some Do, Some Don't: The Decomposition Story

Materials

- ✓ food waste, such as lettuce leaves, an apple core, or potato peels
- ✓ yard waste, such as grass clippings, shredded weeds, or leaves
- ✓ cloth from natural sources, such as cotton or wool
- ✓ synthetic cloth, such as nylon
- ✓ plastic bag or pieces of Styrofoam
- ✓ aluminum foil
- ✓ paper: recycled and new
- ✓ small spade
- ✓ coffee stirrers or craft sticks
- ✓ waterproof pen or pencil
- ✓ soil
- ✓ water
- ✓ plastic containers such as margarine tubs

Some waste materials that we discard are biodegradable. Microorganisms in the soil decompose them, and they become part of Earth's soil and air. Other materials do not decompose and will remain for years in a landfill or as pollution. To find out which substances are biodegradable and which are not, you can bury samples of different materials in warm, damp soil. Some materials you might try include (1) food waste, such as lettuce leaves, an apple core, or potato peels; (2) yard waste, such as grass clippings and shredded weeds or leaves; (3) cloth from natural sources, such as cotton or wool and synthetic cloth, such as nylon; (4) a plastic bag or pieces of Styrofoam; (5) metal, such as aluminum foil; and (6) paper, both recycled and new.

If you have a yard, use a small spade to dig a small hole about 10 cm (4 in) deep for each sample. Put the sample in the hole and cover it up with the dirt you removed. Push a coffee stirrer or craft stick into the center of the covered hole. The stick can be labeled with a waterproof pen or pencil so that you can identify the buried material later when you dig it up. Do this for each sample. If the soil becomes dry, water it from time to time.

If you do not have a yard, place the samples in plastic containers such as margarine tubs. Label the containers, cover each sample with soil (not potting soil), and put them in a warm place. Keep the soil damp, not wet, by adding water occasionally.

After a month, dig up each sample. Which ones show evidence of decomposition? Which ones seem not to have decomposed at all? Cover up the samples once more and check them again after another month or so. Continue to do this for as long as possible. Are there some substances that still show no signs of decomposition after many months in the soil?

Experiment 4.4

Don't Toss It! Compost It!

Materials

✓ **an adult**

✓ two or three 120-L (32-gal) plastic trash cans

✓ bricks

✓ a backyard

✓ drill

✓ pine needles or green twigs

✓ food wastes

✓ 3.5-L (1-gal) plastic container with cover

✓ sink

✓ blender

✓ grass clippings

✓ chopped leaves or straw

✓ elastic cord

✓ shovel or garden fork

✓ garden soil

✓ lumber

✓ wire

✓ hooks and eyes

✓ kitchen waste, weeds, dead flowers, or vegetable leaves

✓ powdered limestone

✓ water

✓ 6 hinges

Organic matter—matter that is or was living—will decompose, provided the bacteria and fungi normally found in soils are present. Some of the bacteria and fungi that decompose organic matter are anaerobic. They do not need oxygen to live, and they can digest plant and animal remains in the absence of air. In addition to moisture and warmth, "bugs" that cause decomposition need carbon as an energy source and nitrogen to make protein for their own cells. Plant matter, such as straw, leaves, and sawdust, can provide carbon. Grass clippings, humus, or green vegetables in garbage can provide the nitrogen.

Since the beginning of agriculture, farmers have spread manure on their soil, buried garbage in their gardens, and plowed green rye grass back into the ground. These materials then decompose, providing new soil and nourishment for plants. But you do not have to be a farmer to compost.

Composting is a way to increase the rate at which organic matter decomposes. Many landfills compost yard wastes and garbage to reduce the volume of material going into the landfill. The compost provides a rich soil that can be sold or given away for use in gardens and flower beds.

You can compost garbage at home. Place a 120-L (32-gal) plastic trash can on four or five bricks in your backyard. The container should have 1-cm (3/8-in) holes about 5 cm (2 in) apart in its sides and bottom. **Ask an adult** to drill these holes for you. Cover the bottom of the container with pine needles or green twigs. This will allow air to reach the waste material that will be in the bottom of the container.

Collect food wastes, except for fatty materials, meat, and bones, in a 3.5-L (1-gal) covered, plastic container beneath the sink. You can collect fruit peels, carrots and potato peels, lettuce, and other plant waste from cooking. Do not include any matter that is not organic. Tear or cut the waste into small pieces before placing it in the container. You might even **ask an adult** to chop the material in a blender. When the container is full, empty it into the large trash can you have prepared. Sprinkle a layer of pine needles, grass clippings, or chopped leaves or straw on the garbage each time you add waste to the large container. Then secure the cover to the container with an elastic cord.

While you are gradually filling the large container, prepare a second one just like the first. Again, **ask an adult** to drill the holes in the sides and bottom. Place the second large container beside the first one. When the first container is full, use a shovel or garden fork to transfer the waste from the first container into the second. The last waste added will then be on the bottom of the new container and the oldest waste on the top. Do not be alarmed to see insects or worms in the waste. They help to decompose and mix the waste.

By the time you have filled the first container again, the waste in the second container may be ready for your garden or flower beds. If it is "done," it will be cool, dark, and crumbly. It should have an earthy odor, not moldy or rotten. If it's not ready, transfer it to a third container identical to the first two. If it appears to be well decomposed, wheel it to your garden, dump it, and mix it with the garden soil.

Although it will take longer for complete decomposition, you can simply bury food wastes about 20 cm (8 in) below the surface of your garden. Dig up the buried waste after several months to see how rapidly it is rotting. Be sure to bury it again when you have finished inspecting it.

Another approach to composting is to build a container like the ones shown in Figure 28 to hold your compost. The wire allows air to reach the decaying matter. The hooks and eyes make it easy to move the compost pile because the fence can be taken apart and reassembled quickly. The larger size will cause the pile to heat up more quickly and increase the rate of decay. Add a cover to prevent animals from reaching the waste.

Start with a depth of about 15 cm (6 in) of organic material (kitchen waste, weeds, dead flowers, grass clippings, or vegetable leaves—no fats, meat, or bones). Add a 5-cm (2-in) layer of rich soil. Then sprinkle on a handful of powdered limestone before repeating the layering process with another layer of organic matter. You might also add wood ashes if you have a fireplace or charcoal ashes from a grill.

If you have enough matter to build a pile 1 m (3 ft) high, you may have useful soil within several months. If you build the compost pile more slowly, it will take longer—a year or more—to convert waste to garden soil. A compost pile that grows slowly doesn't develop enough heat to speed the growth and activity of the microorganisms that cause matter to decompose.

Add water, if necessary, to keep the compost damp but not wet. It should feel like a damp sponge from which water has been squeezed. It may be necessary to poke holes so that moisture and air can reach the inner parts of the pile.

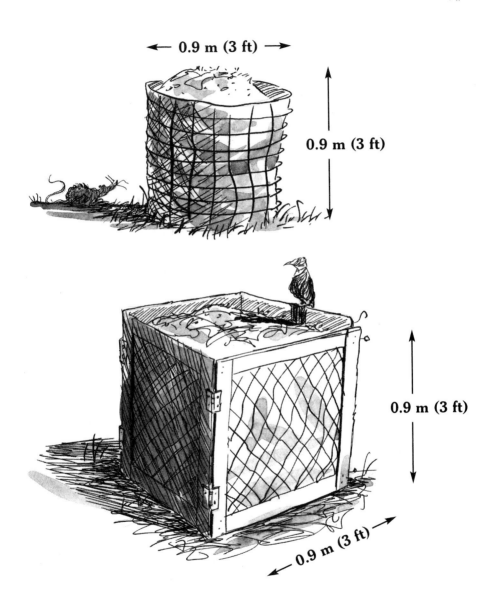

Figure 28.

Plans for two simple compost bins are shown here. Either can be easily moved.

When the original matter has changed in color and consistency, turn the pile over. This is easily done by unhooking the wire fence and moving it so that it is next to the pile. Then use a shovel or garden fork to move the compost pile to its new location. The recently added matter will now be on the bottom of the pile and the original matter will be on top.

Experiment 4.5

Factors that Affect Composting

Materials

✓ **an adult**

✓ 5 large plastic containers

✓ garden soil

✓ food wastes

✓ leaves

✓ water

✓ 10-5-10 fertilizer

✓ blender or food processor

✓ grass clippings

✓ earthworms

✓ thermometer (⁻10°C–110°C)

✓ small garden tool

You can test different ways of composting by changing the materials you put together in miniature compost piles. Obtain five large plastic tubs, each about the size of a 5-gal fish tank (aquarium). Each tub should contain alternate layers of soil 2.5 cm (1 in) deep, organic waste to a depth of 5 cm (2 in), a sprinkling of 10-5-10 fertilizer, and enough water to dampen throughout. Repeat this layering until the tub is filled. In one container, use food wastes (no fat, bones, or meat) as the organic layer. In a second, use chopped leaves as the organic layer. **Ask an adult** to use a blender or food processor to chop the leaves into small pieces. In a third, use grass clippings for the organic layer. In a fourth, use food wastes again but this time **ask an adult** to use a blender or food processor to chop the food into small pieces. In a fifth, use chopped leaves as the organic material, and add a few earthworms to the container. Keep all the tubs in a warm dry place. Add water when necessary to keep the material as damp as a squeezed sponge.

Because these miniature compost piles are so small, their temperatures will not rise as high as those with a large volume. Nevertheless, you can use a thermometer to measure the temperature at the center of each miniature compost pile every day. Which tub gets warmest? After the temperature in a tub reaches a peak and starts to fall, use a small garden tool to mix the compost. This will allow more air to reach the decaying material.

Which organic matter decays faster, food wastes, leaves, or grass clippings? How does chopping the matter into small pieces affect the rate of decay within the pile? What effects do earthworms have on the decay process? After all the miniature compost piles have turned to soil, they can be added to a garden.

Experiment 4.6

The Greenhouse Effect and Global Warming

Materials

✓ 2 identical thermometers
✓ clear plastic container that can be closed
✓ bright sunlight
✓ black paper
✓ an automobile

Air is a mixture of gases. Twenty-one percent of air is oxygen, 78 percent is nitrogen, and almost one percent is argon. There are also small (trace) amounts of carbon dioxide, methane, nitrous oxide, ozone, and other gases, including water vapor. (The concentration of water vapor varies greatly and may be as high as one percent.) These trace gases, particularly carbon dioxide and water vapor, are called greenhouse gases.

About half the radiant energy (light, including infrared and ultraviolet) from the Sun reaches Earth's surface and warms it. The other half is reflected into space by the atmosphere. Of the half that warms Earth's surface, much of it would be radiated right back into space as infrared radiation were it not for the greenhouse gases. These gases, like the glass in a greenhouse, are transparent to short light waves (ultraviolet radiation) from the Sun. However, they absorb much of the longer-wave (infrared) energy released by Earth's surface. By preventing this energy from escaping into space, these gases create a warm blanket that covers Earth. Without these greenhouse gases, Earth would be colder, perhaps too cold to support life. On the other hand, if the concentration of greenhouse gases increases, Earth could become warmer.

You can carry out an experiment that will demonstrate the greenhouse effect. Find two identical thermometers. Place one in a clear plastic container that can be closed. It will serve as the greenhouse. Put the box with the enclosed thermometer in bright sunlight. Place the second thermometer beside the plastic box, as shown in Figure 29. Watch both thermometers for a few minutes. What do you conclude?

Predict what you think will happen if you line the box with black paper and repeat the experiment. Try it. Was your prediction correct?

Here is another way to observe the greenhouse effect. Close the windows of a car that is at rest in sunlight. Half an hour later, return to the car. What do you notice as you enter the vehicle?

Since 1880, the concentration of carbon dioxide in the atmosphere has increased from 290 ppm (parts per million) to 360 ppm, an increase of nearly 25 percent. During that same period of time, Earth's average temperature has increased by about 0.7°C, or 1.25 °F. The increased levels of

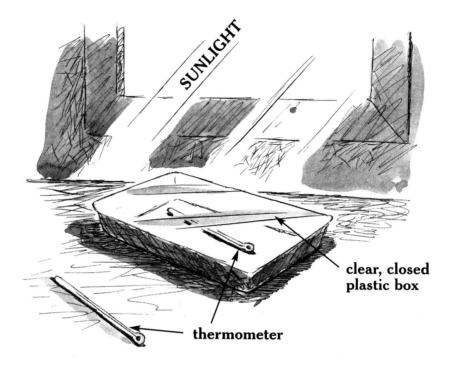

Figure 29.

How does the temperature inside this mini greenhouse compare with the temperature outside the greenhouse?

carbon dioxide in the atmosphere are causing Earth's average temperature to increase. Many scientists believe the increase in atmospheric carbon dioxide is making Earth warmer. This is called global warming.

Chapter 5

Mapping Earth

Maps are scaled drawings of part or all of Earth's surface. A map may show the boundaries of a person's property, a region of wilderness, or the entire world. Road maps, found in almost every car, are the most commonly used maps. They show a bird's-eye view of the relative locations and intersections of roads.

Many maps are based on photographs taken from airplanes. Landmarks on the photographs are matched with known points on the ground whose latitude and longitude are known. Using this data, the maps are drawn and labels added.

The maps you will make are based on measurements and directions established from compass readings and a bench-mark. Such techniques are still used to make maps of properties and to establish boundary lines.

Experiment 5.1

Mapping a Room

Materials

- ✓ bedroom or classroom
- ✓ tape measure
- ✓ ruler
- ✓ pencil
- ✓ sheet of paper, preferably graph paper
- ✓ protractor if graph paper is not available

You can make a map of your bedroom or classroom. First, measure the length and width of the room. Then choose a scale that will allow you to fit the room's dimensions on a sheet of paper. For example, one centimeter on your paper might be used to represent 50 cm of the room's length and width. This would be a scale of 1:50. Or you might use one inch to represent one foot. This would be a 1:12 scale. A protractor will help you to draw right angles. (If you have graph paper, it will make your task easier because the horizontal and vertical lines are at right angles.)

Once you have made the scale drawing of the room's dimensions, how can you add the furniture to your map?

Experiment 5.2

Maps, Magnets, and Earth's Magnetic Field

Materials

- ✓ clear night
- ✓ a partner or two
- ✓ sticks
- ✓ sunny day
- ✓ tape measure or ruler
- ✓ compass
- ✓ thread
- ✓ 2 bar magnets
- ✓ table far from any metal objects
- ✓ white paper
- ✓ pencil
- ✓ iron filings or steel wool and scissors
- ✓ empty spice shaker
- ✓ thin cardboard

In making the map in the previous experiment you probably did not consider how the room was oriented with regard to geographical directions. But directions become very important when maps are made of roads, property boundaries, town and city lines, maps for hikers, and so on. In fact, almost any map will show the direction that is north as well as the map's scale (in/mi, cm/km, in/yd, etc.).

Here are two ways to find the direction we call true north. On a clear night, find the North Star (Polaris; see Experiment 1.5). Because Polaris lies almost directly above Earth's North Pole, it can be used to find true north. Establish a sight line to

Polaris. Have a partner stand under that sight line. Then place two sticks in the ground, one where you are standing and one where your partner is standing. A line from your stake to hers points toward true north (see Figure 30a).

A second method can be done in the daytime. Place a stake in the ground. In the northern hemisphere, the stake's shadow will be shortest when the Sun is due south and at its highest point in the sky. Because the Sun is due south, its shadow will point toward true north. You might think that midday, when the Sun is due south, will occur at noon. But this is seldom the case. The best way to find true north is to wait until the Sun is approaching its highest point in the sky. **(Never look directly at the Sun. It can seriously damage your eyes.)** At that time begin marking the end of the stake's shadow. Continue to mark it at five-minute intervals until you are certain the shadow is growing longer.

Find the shortest shadow by measuring the distances from the stake to the marks you made at the ends of the shadows. A line from the stake to the end of the shortest shadow will point toward true north (see Figure 30b). Of course, in the southern hemisphere the shortest shadow will point toward true south.

Hold a good compass above the line that points toward true north. Unless you live along a line stretching from the panhandle of Florida to the western shore of Lake Superior, you will probably find that the compass needle is *not* parallel to the true-north line you have drawn.

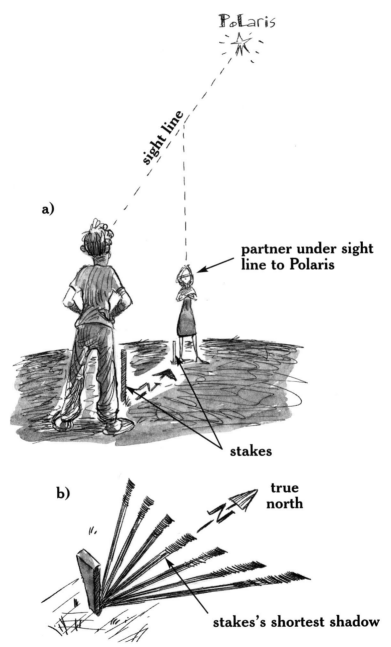

Figure 30.

Finding true north using (a) the North Star (Polaris) and (b) the shortest shadow around midday.

Stand so that you are facing in the direction that the compass needle points. Hand the compass to a partner and ask her to stand several meters away from you. Ask your partner to also face in the direction that the compass needle points. If possible, repeat the process with a third person. You will find that all of you are facing in the same direction. In the same general location, the compass needle always points in the same direction.

Why does a compass needle not point toward true north; that is, toward Earth's North Pole? As you probably know, a compass needle is a magnet that is free to turn. Every magnet has a north-seeking pole and a south-seeking pole. Sometimes the poles are marked with the letters *N* and *S*.

Suspend a bar magnet from a thread. You will see it orient itself so that its north-seeking pole is north of its south-seeking pole. Next, hold one bar magnet close to a second. You will find that the north pole of one magnet attracts the south pole of the other. You will also find that the north poles of the two magnets repel one another, as do the south poles.

The north-seeking poles of all magnets, including compass needles, point in a northerly direction when suspended above Earth's surface. How does a compass needle behave near a bar magnet?

To find out, put a bar magnet on a table far from any metal objects. Place a compass near the magnet's south-seeking (S) pole, as shown in Figure 31a. Notice that the north-seeking

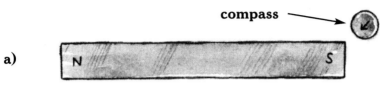

compass

a)

Move compass to here and
draw arrow's direction.

b)

c)

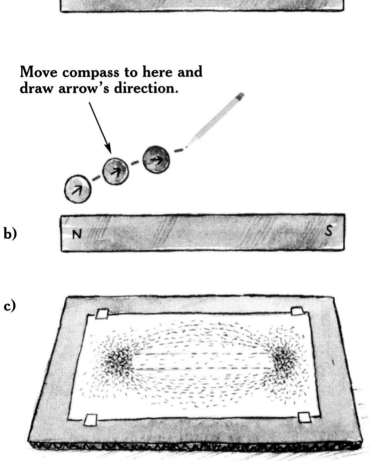

Figure 31.

a) The north-seeking pole of a compass needle is attracted to
the south-seeking pole of a bar magnet. b) A compass can be
used to map the magnetic field around a bar magnet. c) The
bar's magnetic field is revealed by mapping with a compass.

pole of the compass needle is attracted to (points toward) the south-seeking pole of the magnet.

A compass needle's north-seeking pole will point in a particular direction when placed near a magnet. The direction is that of the magnetic field that surrounds the magnet. But the field has a strength as well as a direction. The strength is the force that the field can exert on another magnet or on moving electric charges.

You can map the magnetic field around a bar magnet. Place the magnet on a sheet of white paper. With a pencil, mark the direction that the north-seeking pole of the compass needle points as the compass is moved around the magnet (see Figure 31b). Begin with the compass near the north-seeking pole of the bar magnet. Simply move the compass in the direction the compass needle points to an adjacent position. Repeat this process until you reach the magnet's south-seeking pole.

If you repeat this a number of times, you can map the entire field around the magnet. However, you can map the field more easily with iron filings. These small pieces of iron behave as if they were tiny compass needles. You can probably borrow some iron filings from a science teacher or buy some at a hobby shop. Or you can make your own by using scissors to cut part of a roll of steel wool into tiny pieces over a sheet of paper. Use the paper to pour the particles into an empty spice shaker.

Once you have some iron filings, tape a sheet of white paper to a thin sheet of cardboard. Place the cardboard on a bar magnet. Then sprinkle some iron filings over the paper. Tap the cardboard gently. The filings will align themselves like tiny compass needles, revealing the field lines about the bar magnet (see Figure 31c).

Earth's magnetic field looks much like the field you have just mapped. This would suggest that Earth acts as if it contained a huge bar magnet. Suppose you took a compass to Boothia Peninsula, north of Hudson Bay, about 1,200 miles from Earth's geographic North Pole. There, at about 76 degrees latitude, 100 degrees west longitude, you would find that the north-seeking pole of the compass needle points straight down. You would be standing over one of Earth's magnetic poles. Is the magnetic pole under Boothia Peninsula a north-seeking or a south-seeking pole? How would you know?

At a point in Antarctica near Dumont d'Urville, at about 67 degrees latitude, 140 degrees east longitude, you would be about 1,200 miles from Earth's South Pole. There you would find a compass needle's north-seeking pole points straight up. Is Earth's magnetic pole in Antarctica a north-seeking or a south-seeking pole? How would you know?

You can see now why a compass needle seldom points toward true north. Earth's magnetic and geographic poles are about 1,200 miles apart. A compass near Boston, Massachusetts, will point about 15 degrees west of true north. A compass near San Diego, California, will point about 15 degrees east of true north. There is a line stretching from the

Florida Panhandle to the western edge of Lake Superior along which a compass needle *does* point toward true north. Such a line is called an agonic line. The difference between true north and magnetic north as indicated by a compass is called the magnetic declination. However, Earth's magnetism is constantly changing. Therefore, charts showing the angles of magnetic declination on Earth's surface have to be revised frequently.

Using a compass and the true north line you drew, estimate the magnetic declination where you live.

Science Project Ideas

- Some scientists believe that birds and other animals use Earth's magnetic field to guide them as they migrate or move from place to place. What evidence can be offered to support this idea?

- If you lived south of the equator, how would you find true north?

Experiment 5.3

Mapping an Outdoor Area

Materials

✓ thin piece of wood about 30 cm × 45 cm (12 in × 18 in)	✓ cardboard
	✓ tape
	✓ large sheet of paper
✓ stick about 2.5 cm × 2.5 cm × 90 cm (1 in × 1 in × 36 in)	✓ pencil
	✓ magnetic compass
✓ 2 right-angle metal braces and screws	✓ straight pins
	✓ ruler
✓ lawn, ball field, school, or similar area	✓ notebook
	✓ a partner
✓ sticks	✓ tape measure

To map a large outdoor area, a mapping table is useful. You can make one from a thin piece of wood about 30 cm × 45 cm (12 in × 18 in), a stick about 2.5 cm × 2.5 cm × 90 cm (1 in × 1 in × 36 in), two right-angle metal braces, and screws (see Figure 32a).

A lawn, ball field, or school yard would make a reasonable area to map. Choose a point at one corner of the area as a place to start. Assume there is a benchmark at that point. (A benchmark is a solid marker such as a short concrete post for which the latitude and longitude have been established. You

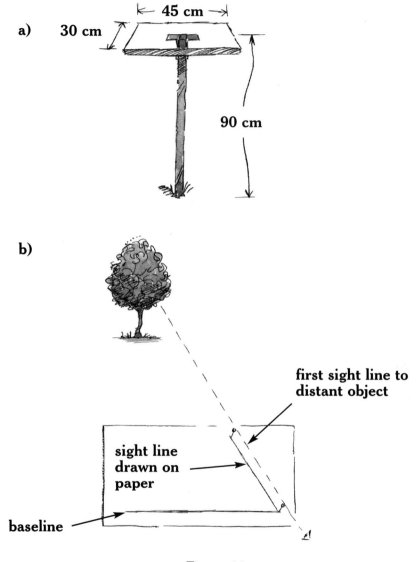

Figure 32.

a) A mapping table will be helpful in making a map of an area. You can make one quite easily. b) From one end of a baseline, use pins to make and draw sight lines to distant objects in the area you are mapping.

may actually be able to find one at the corner of a piece of property.) If there is no benchmark, insert a stick to represent one at the corner you have chosen.

To map the area, you will make two sight lines to various objects from opposite ends of a baseline. Place the mapping table at the point you have chosen as a benchmark. It will serve as one end of the baseline. Cover the table with a sheet of cardboard and tape it in place. Then tape a large sheet of paper to the cardboard. Outline the position of the compass near one corner of the paper and leave it in place. On the paper, mark the direction of magnetic north according to the compass needle. Should the compass be moved, it can always be realigned from the mark and outline.

Do you know the magnetic declination? If you do, mark the direction of true north on your map.

Use two pins to mark a sight line from a point near one corner of the paper to some identifiable object on the other side of the area you are mapping (see Figure 32b). Draw the sight line on the paper using a ruler and the pins. Repeat the process for a number of other objects within the area. Each time, check to be sure that the sight lines you drew earlier are still aligned properly. The object to which the sight line is directed can be identified by writing a number on the line. A record of the number and the object it identifies can be kept in a notebook.

Use your compass and sight lines to determine the direction of each object relative to magnetic north. For example, if the sight line is 15 degrees east of the direction indicated by the compass needle, its direction (bearing) is 15 degrees east of magnetic north. What is its direction relative to true north?

After you have drawn a number of sight lines to objects within the area you wish to map, ask a partner to stand at a point, say 30 m (100 ft), toward another corner of the area to be mapped. Draw a sight line from your present position to the point where the person stands. Place a stake at the second position and move the mapping table there. The compass needle should point to the same mark you made earlier to indicate magnetic north. Sight back along the sight line you just made to the mapping table's first position to be sure the mapping table is correctly oriented. The distance between these two positions constitutes the baseline you will use in preparing the map. The line between these two points on the paper corresponds to the two stakes in the ground. But, how far apart should those two points be on the paper?

The scale must be such that the map will fit on the paper. For example, suppose you choose to let one centimeter on the map equal one meter of ground (a scale of 1:100). If the ends of the baseline are 30 m apart, set the second pin 30 cm from the first. Use that second pin and another to sight on the object that will require the greatest change in direction relative to the original sight line you drew to it from the benchmark. For example, if you moved left to establish your baseline, sight on the object farthest to the right. Does the point you chose to represent the end of the baseline on the paper allow the new sight line to cross the older one? If it does, your scale will work. If it doesn't, shorten the baseline on the paper by choosing a scale with a greater ratio. For example, try letting 0.5 cm = 1.0 m (a scale of 1:200).

Once you have a workable scale and the mapping table is properly positioned, draw new sight lines from this end of the baseline to each of the objects you sighted before. Be sure to check the table's orientation before and after you make each sight line.

When you finish, you will see that you have made a series of triangles. The base of each triangle is the same for all of them; it is the baseline on the paper. The sides of the triangles are the sight lines you drew to each object from opposite ends of the baseline. Each object on the map is at the apex of the individual triangles (see Figure 33). You might like to extend the baseline and make a third sight line to each object.

Use the map you are making and a ruler to predict the distances to each of the objects from each end of the baseline. Then measure the distances with a tape measure. How do the measured distances compare with your predictions based on the map? Finally, predict the distances between the objects using the map. Then measure the distances. How do the predicted and actual distances compare?

If your map is accurate, you can erase the sight lines and write the scale ratio on the map. You now have a map of the area.

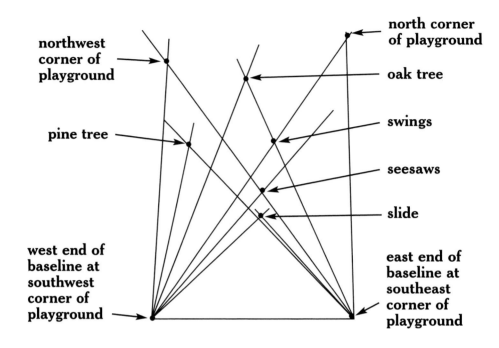

Figure 33.

Sight lines drawn from the two ends of a baseline can be used to map a playground.

Science Project Ideas

- What is a contour map? Devise a model to show how contour maps are made.

- Make a contour map of a small area near your home.

Appendix

SCIENCE SUPPLY COMPANIES

Carolina Biological Supply Company
2700 York Road
Burlington, NC 27215-3398
(800) 334-5551
http://www.carolina.com

Connecticut Valley Biological
Supply Company
82 Valley Road
P.O. Box 326
Southampton, MA 01073
(800) 628-7748
http://www.ctvalleybio.com

Delta Education
80 Northwest Boulevard
P.O. Box 3000
Nashua, NH 03061-3000
(800) 442-5444
http://www.delta-education.com

Edmund Scientifics
60 Pearce Avenue
Tonawanda, NY 14150-6711
(800) 728-6999
http://scientificsonline.com

Educational Innovations, Inc.
362 Main Avenue
Norwalk, CT 06851
(888) 912-7474
http://www.teachersource.com

Fisher Science Education
4500 Turnberry Drive
Hanover Park, IL 60133
(800) 955-1177
https://www1.fishersci.com/education/
index.jsp

Frey Scientific
100 Paragon Parkway
Mansfield, OH 44903
(800) 225-3739
http://www.freyscientific.com

NASCO-Fort Atkinson
901 Janesville Avenue
P.O. Box 901
Fort Atkinson, WI 53538-0901
(800) 558-9595
http://www.nascofa.com

NASCO-Modesto
4825 Stoddard Road
P.O. Box 3837
Modesto, CA 95352-3837
(800) 558-9595
http://www.nascofa.com

Sargent-Welch/VWR Scientific
P.O. Box 5229
Buffalo Grove, IL 60089-5229
(800) 727-4386
http://sargentwelch.com/default.asp?

Science Kit & Boreal Laboratories
777 East Park Drive
P.O. Box 5003
Tonawanda, NY 14150
(800) 828-7777
http://sciencekit.com

Ward's Natural Science
P.O. Box 92912
Rochester, NY 14692-9012
(800) 962-2660
http://www.wardsci.com

Further Reading

Bombaugh, Ruth. *Science Fair Success, Revised and Expanded.* Springfield, N.J.: Enslow Publishers, Inc., 1999.

Brimmer, Larry Dane. *Mountains.* Danbury, Conn.: Children's Press, 2001.

Gardner, Robert. *Science Fair Projects—Planning, Presenting, Succeeding.* Springfield, N.J.: Enslow Publishers, Inc., 1998.

———— *Science Project Ideas About Space Science, Revised Edition.* Berkeley Heights, N.J.: Enslow Publishers, Inc., 2002.

VanCleave, Janice. *A+ Projects in Earth Science: Winning Experiments for Science Fairs and Extra Credit.* New York: John Wiley & Sons, 1998.

Internet Addresses

The Exploratorium. Exploratorium Home Page.
http://www.exploratorium.edu

Reeko's Mad Scientist Lab—Educational Experiments.
http://www.spartechsoftware.com/reeko

Yahooligans!—Science and Nature: Experiments and Activities.
http://www.yahooligans.com/science_and_nature/
Experiments_and_Activities

Index